HERE ARE JUST ⬧ W9-CMB-362 QUESTIONS THAT IRA COBLEIGH ANSWERS FOR YOU!

—Where do the best bets for big profits lie—in high-priced or inexpensive issues?

—What special industry groupings are destined for rapid expansion in the last third of the seventies?

—What specific companies look like the top winners in the year to come?

—What vital checkpoints should I look for in any stock I am interested in?

—How has the rise of institutional investment altered the whole concept of market strategy?

—Can the "little guy" still make a fast fortune on the Street?

We will answer that last question right here. The answer is YES! Because that is what this most famous of all investment guides is all about.

IRA U. COBLEIGH is a consulting economist, financial editor, and the author of many books and monographs on investment opportunities and economics. He was, for twenty-three years, Feature Editor of *The Commercial & Financial Chronicle;* since 1969, he has been Associate Editor of *The Market Chronicle.* Other books by Mr. Cobleigh include *All about Stocks, How to Choose a Growth Stock, All about Credit,* and *The Coming 300% Rise in Silver.* Mr. Cobleigh is a lecturer at The New School for Social Research, has made frequent appearances on various radio and television programs, and was the host of the early morning NBC-TV show, "The Stock Market: Guidelines for Gains." He is a director of nine corporations and a consultant to several gold and silver mining companies.

SIGNET and MENTOR Books of Special Interest

HAPPINESS IS A STOCK THAT DOUBLES IN A YEAR

1977 EDITION

by

Ira U. Cobleigh

A BERNARD GEIS ASSOCIATES BOOK

A SIGNET BOOK
NEW AMERICAN LIBRARY
TIMES MIRROR

Charts in this book by Susan MacFarlane, Technical Staff of
John Magee, Inc., Springfield, Massachusetts.

SIGNET, SIGNET CLASSICS, MENTOR, PLUME AND MERIDIAN BOOKS
are published by The New American Library, Inc.,
1301 Avenue of the Americas, New York, New York 10019.

FIRST SIGNET PRINTING, DECEMBER, 1976

. 3 4 5 6 7 8 9

PRINTED IN THE UNITED STATES OF AMERICA

Contents

Introduction

This book, *Happiness Is a Stock that Doubles in a Year* (1977 edition), is the successor to a book by the same title and author, published (and a national bestseller) in 1967. The book spotlighted a surprisingly high number of stocks that actually doubled. In fact, of the 45 stocks listed, 31 percent actually doubled or better within a year. One stock increased sevenfold; all gained to some degree except one, which lost a point and a half.

Since then, a number of significant changes—both in the economic climate of the United States and in the attitudes of brokers and investors—point up the need for a current book offering updated guidelines to those enterprising individuals who are eager to take on riskier and more volatile securities in their quests for above-average market gains. What are some of these changes in climate and attitudes that make necessary a new set of tactics, and new criteria for security selection, if one is to achieve a swift expansion in net worth?

Since 1971, the United States has gone off the gold exchange standard; the dollar, until August 15, 1971, worth 1/35th of an ounce of gold, no longer has any direct relationship or link to gold. The dollar is a floating currency—a "greenback"—and in common with all other paper money in history is likely to display a continued decline in purchasing power, because there is no limit on its issuance.

This predictable deterioration and devaluation of our currency is fueling a powerful and possibly even uncontrollable force in our economic environment—inflation. This was reported at 11.2 percent in 1974, dropped down to around 7.6 percent in 1975, down again to about 6 percent in 1976, but appears certain to ascend again to double digits in 1977 and beyond, because of: (1) debts in all categories which keep reaching new highs (as this was written, the Federal debt ceiling was raised to $624 billion!); and (2) huge government deficits—$45.2 billion in fiscal 1975 and $65.6 billion in fiscal 1976. Anyone who seriously believes that we have licked inflation is in need of a psychiatrist.

One would think that another influence on inflation would be the notable nationwide decline in political and corporate morality that we've seen over the last few years—a downward progression from Spiro Agnew's resignation to Watergate to Gerry Ford's unpardonable pardon of Richard Nixon, accompanied by disclosure of dozens of illegal corporate contributions to the Nixon reelection campaign, not to mention the international bribery involved in foreign business solicitation by such corporate greats as Lockheed, Northrup, Boeing, Grumman, Exxon, Mobil, Gulf, etcetera. We must have become a very callous nation, however, because all of these corporate exposures and unveilings of shady payoffs, not heretofore revealed in published financial reports, had only ripple effects on the market quotations of the stocks in the companies involved.

Then there has been a structural change in the market itself. Transactions on the New York Stock Exchange are now over 70 percent institutional, and it is not at all uncommon to have over 200 orders a day executed in lots of 10,000 shares or more. Compare this to 1968, when New York Stock Exchange transactions were 55 percent individual.

What this all means is that now the major nationwide brokerage firms are concentrating on the big buyers, confining their research, for the most part, to the giant companies with millions of shares outstanding, the ones enjoying very broad and active trading markets. If you walk into a branch of one of these big brokerage firms with only $500 or $1,000 to invest, you will get only a stamp-sized welcome mat. If you request information or a current analytical report on a little-known or regional company, it will probably be unavailable. Further, the customer's broker may suggest that your purchases be confined to the issues of the big companies on which his firm has prepared reports. In this way, you may be subtly steered away from speculation in some smaller, early-phase company you had in mind, one possibly traded in the Over-the-Counter market but which might with luck become another Polaroid, American Home Products, or Tropicana.

It is to fill this broad information gap, and to provide a useful approach to speculation in shares otherwise neglected or overlooked, that this book was especially written.

As for customer attitudes, since 1973, due to the availability of good bonds yielding variously between 8 and 10 percent, many individuals who would otherwise have been stock buyers have been salting their surplus funds away in bonds. Stock yields on the 30 Dow-Jones Industrials, currently about 4 percent, have appeared relatively unrewarding. There is a quite well-documented theory that good, seasoned common stocks should provide a long-term return of about 9 percent annually (combining dividends with capital appreciation). When individuals can obtain a 9 percent yield in AA bonds, with minimum risk of market decline, they opt for these bonds, perhaps vividly remembering the steep stock declines of 1974–1975.

Of the 28 million reported stockholders in America today, it is reasonable to conjecture that over 20 percent (or around 6 million) are at heart speculators who yearn for market action and who are far more interested in exciting capital gains than in merely tucking their money away at interest. For them, even under the changed conditions we have touched upon, it is still possible through a fortunate combination of market knowledge, reliable sources of information, a sense of timing, and a little luck, to buy stocks that double. The Dow-Jones Average itself doubled (from lowest point to top) in 1932 and 1933; in any bull market year, 5 percent of the issues on the New York Stock Exchange may double—and over 20 percent on the American Stock Exchange! Some few will perform spectacularly, scoring gains up to 500 percent. The opportunities are there if you can spot them.

The desire to double one's money is indeed an attractive objective and, if attained, can both build one's bank account and enhance a sense of personal achievement. Nothing is more fun than to go to a cocktail party and, when the conversation turns to "the market," smilingly mention the stocks you own that doubled, explaining how you came to pick them out.

Your aim to double your money in lively stocks is quite attainable, even though only a modest percentage of the issues you select for that purpose may reach the goal. (That doesn't mean, however, that the others will lose money.) Don't expect the moon—even the best batters in baseball make a hit only one time in three, and the leading horse handicappers usually pick only one winner out of three.

You'll have a lot of fun screening, buying, and watching your stocks. The endeavors will add zest to your life and, with good fortune, keep you in Cadillacs, cruisers, and condominiums. Good luck! Cast your bread upon the waters —and it may come back a club sandwich!

Note

A problem connected with this and every book discussing marketable securities is that every quotation given in the manuscript becomes technically out of date the next day. Fortunately, this is not generally an important factor. Nine times out of ten, the variation will not be significant. What counts is the quotation on the stock a year from the time you buy it. If my track record is as good this time around as it was the first time, your chances are excellent. With all this, I must add the necessary disclaimer that no actual endorsement or guarantee is made of any of the stocks listed in this book, and nothing herein is to be considered as an offer or inducement to buy, sell, or hold any security.

HAPPINESS IS
A STOCK
THAT DOUBLES
IN A YEAR

Chapter I

How and Where to Look for Stocks that Can Double

Happiness is the name of this book, so we should start out with a definition. An ancient Chinese proverb defines happiness as, "Something to do, someone to love, and something to hope for." That description applies as well to the stock market. The "something to do" is gathering useful information about promising securities and prevailing economic trends, and watching eagerly the daily market movement in the stocks you own. There's no "someone to love" in Wall Street, but there is some*thing* to love—a soaring stock registered in your name. And, of course, the essence of speculation is "something to hope for"—the excitement of a series of gains that document the wisdom of your security decisions and the excellence of your timing in selling before profits melt. You can't buy minks and Eldorados on paper profits!

Zeroing in on Doublers—
A Different Technique

Most books on investment emphasize safety, marketability, diversification, and income dependability, with capital gain as a derivative but not a major objective. Our approach is entirely different—a neat capital gain, one that at least doubles your money, is our goal. To achieve that, it is not important to pay close attention to diversification or dividend rates, or even to follow in any detail the performance of seasoned securities and such blue chips as comprise the portfolios of bank trust departments, pension funds, insurance companies, and major investment trusts. Professional managers of such portfolios are content with capital gains in any year equal to those in the Dow-Jones Industrial Average. Because our goal is more ambitious, the procedures traditionally used by these institutional investors are simply not effective. In fact, one of the impediments to success in zeroing in on stocks for doubling is the practice of major brokerage houses and investment banking firms to concentrate their efforts and the facilities they provide on business with institutions.

With volume on the New York Stock Exchange reaching on occasion more than 30 million shares a day, and over 70 percent of the trading done by institutions on that exchange, the research of brokerage houses is in most cases limited to the large, seasoned, national and international companies, which gross in the hundreds of millions annually, have many millions of shares outstanding, and enjoy high-volume daily trading activity. These shares, regularly bought and sold in 10,000 share lots, generate such substantial commission revenues for the big wire houses that it simply is not worth their while to solicit and handle the tradings of modest individual investors.

Yet it is this same individual who is the avid speculator, willing to risk his or her funds on low-priced shares which may be light-years away from any dividends, or to speculate in the equities of new and unseasoned companies with small capitalizations, whose shares trade inactively in the OTC market. The big brokerage houses seldom do extensive research on these second- or third-tier companies, which is why I said earlier that this book is intended to fill a very large gap. There *are* a few daring people left in our homogenized society.

The Necessary Sources of Information

The first problem facing the avid speculator is where to get the information he or she needs. With some 40,000 different issues traded in American security markets each day, including about 7,000 which are traded quite actively on the various exchanges and OTC, where can one get the facts about obscure, small, or regional companies with publicly held shares and trading markets, however thin? Where can one get enough material to provide the basis for a decision to buy or not to buy stock in a particular company?

The most obvious sources are the financial sections of major metropolitan dailies—the New York *Times*, Chicago *Tribune*, Denver *Post*, Los Angeles *Times*, Miami *Herald*,

Philadelphia *Inquirer,* Houston *Post,* and others. These newspapers regularly print not only quotation tables but also news items and, often, special articles on public companies. More complete than any of these, however, for eager investors, is the daily coverage supplied by the *Wall Street Journal.*

Among financial magazines, *Barron's, Forbes, The Financial World, Dun's Review, The OTC Review, Investment Dealers' Digest, The Financial Weekly,* and *The Market Chronicle* are all excellent sources of current financial information. Among the investment services, Standard & Poor's publish not only complete security manuals but also updated fact sheets on hundreds of companies. These sheets may be acquired directly from S & P or from brokerage firms that supply them to individual clients on request. Value Line also publishes regularly updated sheets on hundreds of companies, as well as useful charts recording their market performance over a considerable period of time. Moody's and Dun and Bradstreet provide comprehensive investors' services.

There are dozens of other investment advisory services that publish weekly or monthly market letters, along with special studies or reports on securities they have researched and that they particularly favor.

If you hear about a company that sounds interesting, you can always write to its headquarters and request its latest annual report and most recent quarterly statement. You should also ask them to send you their Securities and Exchange Commission Report 10-K, which contains more detailed information than is generally provided in the company's more public-relations-oriented material.

But whatever you do, don't wait for someone to mention a stock. Keep your eyes open for a new product, service, or trend that may swiftly and favorably affect the fortunes of a particular company.

All these media provide the reservoirs of the information you seek. Read all the respected financial publications regularly and send for reports on the companies advertised in them. You simply cannot play the market successfully by ear. For example, you will seldom acquire a winner by putting in an order for a stock somebody mentioned at a social gathering, as a "zinger." Quite possibly the person who name-dropped the stock may be "shilling" it (i.e., getting people to buy either a dubious stock or one that a group of insiders is eager to unload).

In any event, be adequately informed before you risk

your hard-earned money. Tips, hearsay, or rumor are not enough. Even if you learn that a person of substance whom you respect has "bought a bale" of Zilchboom Electronics common, don't rush to the phone. The issue may already have advanced to far more than it is worth—and be about to descend!

WHERE NOT TO LOOK

In our quest for stocks that appear likely in a given time period to outperform the rest of the market, there are whole groups of securities that we exclude in advance from consideration—long-seasoned, dividend-paying securities and high-priced blue chips that historically and mathematically have small chance of doubling within a year's time. For example, A T & T, with more stockholders than any other company (close to three million), has never doubled in a year and remains unlikely to do so. The same may be said of most electric utility shares—Pacific Gas & Electric, Florida Power and Light, Commonwealth Edison, Public Service Electric and Gas, etcetera. While any of these may report advances in net profits, or pleasing dividend increases in a given year, this news will seldom be reflected in any dramatic price uptrend, because: (1) there are so many millions of shares outstanding in each instance; and (2) changes in fortunes of utilities are seldom dramatic enough to attract active speculative buying. The only big utility stock we can recall that varied by over 100 percent in a year recently is Con Edison, which passed its dividend in 1974 and ranged between 5 and 21½ in 1974, and 7½ and 15 in 1975.

Other stable market groups that generally afford meager prospects for soaring are mature bank stocks, life insurance company shares, and the exalted companies that make up the Dow-Jones Average. Further, it appears most unlikely in the bull market of 1976 that such already high-priced blue chip dividend-payers as Coca-Cola, Johnson and Johnson, IBM, General Motors, United States Steel, Merck, Wrigley, or Time, Inc. would double in price, although high-grade equities such as these may record price variations of 25 percent or more in an average market year. If a stock sells above 50 and at a P/E multiple over 16, it's probably not on your shopping list.

Needless to say, many stocks of this type are fine investments for certain purposes. But you bought this book because you are interested in doubling your money in a year, and these stocks are not the answers to your prayers.

WHERE TO LOOK

What we've been saying is that the institutional-type conservative stock is seldom a dazzling performer, although it may advance moderately in price year after year.

The market sectors where doublers are found more generally include: (1) smaller and less well-known companies; (2) newer and rapidly growing industries; (3) tired companies in a turnaround; (4) companies featuring exciting new products, services, or patents; (5) innovators attracting speculators with such novelties, fads, or fashions as snowmobiles, skateboards, citizens' band radios, ballpoint pens, denim clothes, crockery pots, and the like; (6) mining and oil companies that luck out with their drill bits and discover new ore bodies or oilfields; (7) "merger bait" properties; (8) cyclical companies—coppers, land developers, building materials; (9) distress or even bankrupt companies; (10) enterprises priced so low that any substantial buying may attract migrant speculators; (11) new issues; (12) reorganized company shares; (13) special situations; (14) enterprises revived by new money or management; and (15) inflation hedges. Stocks that perform sensationally will almost invariably qualify somewhere on this list, often in more than one category. In all of these sectors, however, the most important factors to propel stocks upward are: (1) *sustained and above-average growth* in profits: or (2) visible and imminent prospects for substantial rise in profits.

MARKET CLIMATE

The overall market climate is also an important consideration. Looking back over the decade, you'll notice that there were always some stocks that doubled. But the number that gain in bear markets is meager. In the bull market year of 1965, there were 55 stocks that, at the end of the year, were selling at 100 percent or more above their opening January quotations on the New York Stock Exchange, and 110 issues that doubled (under the same rule) on the American Stock Exchange. That two to one relationship between AMEX and NYSE is now improved, due to: (1) the greater number of lower-priced shares listed on AMEX in the past decade; and (2) the fact that approximately 70 percent of the volume on the AMEX is generally in trading by individuals, making it the home ground of the speculator.

From the above, we should not conclude that you should never speculate "for the rise" in bear markets, but rather that your prospects for success are far greater when you swim with a rising tide. The best time to buy either long shots or blue chips is, of course, in the early phase of a bull market. As the whole market advances, and the better issues move up out of reach, there's a constant downdrift of speculators to progressively less sturdy equities, the ones selling in the lower price ranges. This is due to one of the oft-repeated beliefs of seasoned traders. In a favorable market climate, the lower-priced stocks, regardless of their relative merits, will record greater percentage gains than those purchased at higher levels. For example, a stock selling at 50 is far more likely to double than one selling at 100; a stock at 20 has definitely superior gainful potentials than one at 40; a share at 10 is speculatively more promising than one bought at 20.

Investment bankers, in their endeavors to popularize the equity of a substantial client industrial company, seem to think that between $20 and $30 is the ideal trading range for a mature, dividend-paying, listed equity—high enough to be above a speculative classification and low enough to attract income-minded buyers and to expand the number of round-lot (100 share) owners. Further, stocks in the $20 to $30 range are less alluring to "in and out" traders. Thus the company will acquire many more permanent stockholders, have less annual expense in transferring stock on the company's books, and can build up a dependable reservoir of capital for any future "rights offering" to share owners. This was the motivation for splitting "Telephone" 3 for 1 a few years back—to bring the issue into a more popular price range. You'll note that stock splits, which occur rather frequently in bull markets, generally wind up with the "when issued" new shares, trading somewhere near the $30 price.

This pricing information is useful for our purposes not only as a guide to optimum buying ranges but also as a clue as to a rewarding selling price. For example, if a stock has moved from $15 to $30, one reason to sell it might be because at $30 the number of people interested in buying it may fall off, and it may lose its upward momentum.

There is a tendency to think that when the Dow Average is high, all the best opportunities have been lost. This is not so. In bull market tops, the Dow multiple has exceeded 16. That being the case, there should be a lot of lively upbound stocks still available while the Dow Average is moving up to 1,600 (a 16-time multiple of $100). Further, there is a significant group of securities analysts and economists believing that the Dow, even at 1,600, would understate the value of stocks in terms of devalued dollars. Stock prices should go higher because the denominator of evaluation, the dollar itself, has been going down for years. If the dollar buys today 40 percent less than it did ten years ago, then the Dow-Jones at 2,000 might not overvalue stock in terms of 1967 dollars.

Furthermore, the prospects for continued inflation are—unfortunately—all on our side so far as an additional thrust in market prices is concerned. There are always opportunities lurking in Wall Street, awaiting only the probing and perception of diligent speculators. With 40,000 issues to chose from, there's bound to be a batch of winners.

Since December, 1974, General Motors rose from 28 to 73⅞; Ford from 28¾ to 60⅞ since October, 1974; and Chrysler from a 1974 low of 7 to 22⅜. At the end of 1974, Dow Chemical was 55 (now 44⅝); Union Camp 39 (now 63⅞); and International Paper, 35¾ (now 70¼). It's time for the second and third team to "take over."

What about 1976? Just within the first 190 days, Gladding Corporation common rose from 2½ to 10¾ and Automated Radio from 2⅝ to 9⅞. Both of these dazzlers trade on the AMEX; both were the swift beneficiaries of the current boom in Citizen Band radios. They document our theory and then some!

Gladding trebled in less than three months. Let's go out and find some more like that!

Chapter II

Doublers in 1975— and What They Teach Us

As you are by now aware, the market objectives set forth in this book differ notably from those of institutional portfolio managers, who seek equities of quality and income stability, or those of the average customers' broker who solicits your consideration of a quite limited list of securities researched by, or carrying the recommendation of, his firm. In fact, only bold, daring, and optimistic individuals would even consider the doubling of capital as a primary and plausible market objective.

Since our goals are different, our techniques must also be different. And indeed they are! In our quest for stocks that can double, we should be able to get some constructive ideas by reviewing a representative group of stocks that have doubled in recent markets. As we will explain in detail in the next chapter, it is the lower-priced stocks that are historically the ones most likely to double. Where are these to be found in volume? The New York Stock Exchange, native habitat of elegant blue chips, is obviously not the best place to look, although three dozen or more issues listed there will double in the average year. Where 70 percent of the buying is institutional, as on NYSE, we would expect the accent to be on investment stature and dividends, and not on price volatility.

A more natural habitat for double-winners is the American Stock Exchange. There the climate is more hospitable to less well-known and newer companies, operating in a trading arena where 70 percent of the buying is for individual accounts, and with 1,218 issues to choose from.

The OTC market is an all-embracing arena of lower-priced shares, but there we often encounter a problem of limited marketability. If you want to buy a given issue, offerings may be thin, gaps between bid and asked prices may

8

be wide, and purchase of even a few hundred shares may drive up the price. Contrariwise, when it's time to sell, liquidation may be difficult, bids tentative or fading, and your big selling question may be, "To whom?"

We therefore concluded that the AMEX is probably the most satisfactory securities market for our purposes. And viewing the performance record of AMEX in 1975 convinces us of the wisdom of that conclusion.

The year 1975 was hardly a glamorous year in Wall Street, yet it did generate 200 doublers on AMEX. To qualify as a doubler, we decided that a stock had to sell on the last trading day of the year at a price at least 100 percent higher than its price the preceding January. This definition arbitrarily excluded a number of stocks that, between their low and highs, gained 100 percent during the year but ended the year at a lower level.

A tabulation of the year's trading, supplied here in Table I, catalogs the 200 issues on AMEX doubling in 1975 out of a total of 1,218 issues listed at the end of the year.

TABLE I

AMERICAN STOCK EXCHANGE DOUBLERS

A tabulation of American Stock Exchange common stock issues that doubled in value from the first trading day (January 2) to the last business day (December 31) in the 1975 calendar year. This group consists of 197 common stock issues and three warrants.

In preparing this tabulation, the lowest sale and/or bid quotation of January 2, 1975, was compared with the highest sale and/or bid of December 31, 1975.

The letter "B" indicates a bid price; all other figures are sales prices.

The prices of two issues, Miller-Wohl and Plantronics, were adjusted to reflect a two for one split in 1975.

Stock	Lowest sale or bid price Jan. 2, 1975	Highest sale or bid price Dec. 31, 1975
A & E Plastik Pak Co.	2⅛	4⅜
Acme Precision Products	¾ B	1½
Action Industries, Inc.	2⅛	4½
Adams-Russell Co.	¾	2
Aero-Flow Dynamics, Inc.	2⅛	4⅝
Aiken Industries, Inc.	1⅜ B	3
Alba-Waldensian, Inc.	⅞	2⅝
Altamil Corp.	1⅝ B	3¾
AMAX Warrants 1977	4	8
American Maize Products		
Class A	7¾	17¾
Class B	8⅛	16¾
Anken Industries	1½ B	3⅝
Askin Service Corp.	¼ B	¾
Astrex, Inc	1	2
Atlas Corporation Perpetual Warrants	1½ B	3¼
Aydin Corporation	1½	4⅜
Banner Industries, Inc.	1⅞	4¼
Basin Petroleum Corp.	4⅜	9¾
Belscot Retailers, Inc.	¾ B	1⅝
Benrus Corp.	1⅝ B	3¾
Bergen Brunswig Corp.	2¼	6¼
Bluebird, Inc.	1¾	3⅝
Bowne & Co., Inc.	4¼ B	9½
Bro-Dart Industries	⅝ B	2⅛ B
Brooks & Perkins, Inc.	4¼	9⅛
Burgess Industries, Inc.	1⅛	3¼
CMT Industries, Inc.	1⅜ B	3¼
CRS Design Associates	3 B	6¼
Cablecom General, Inc.	1⅝	5½
Cagle's Inc.	1¾	4¼
Canadian Homestead Oils, Ltd.	2⅛	4⅞
Canadian Merrill, Ltd.	1⅞	5⅜
Caressa, Inc.	2¼	5½
Child World, Inc.	3⅛	11¾
Clarke-Gravely Corp.	4	8¼
Clarkson Industries, Inc.	2⅝	7
Coachmen Industries, Inc.	3¼ B	22⅞
Coleman Co., Inc.	5⅜	12¾
Concord Fabrics Inc.	1⅛ B	4⅞
Condec Corp.	2	5¾

Stock	Lowest sale or bid price Jan. 2, 1975	Highest sale or bid price Dec. 31, 1975
Conroy, Inc.	1 B	2½
Courtaulds, Ltd.	1⅛ B	2¹⁵⁄₁₆ B
Cox Cable Communications	4⅞ B	13⅜
Craig Corp.	2	8½
Data Products Corp.	2⅛	5
De Rose Industries, Inc.	½	1
Dillard Dept Stores, Inc.	7⅜ B	16¼
Drug Fair, Inc.	4½	10⅛
Dynell Electronics Corp.	2¼	5½
Edmos Corp.	1	2⅛
Edo Corp.	2⅝	7¾
Edwards (A G) & Sons	4⅛	9⅞
Elcor Chemical Corp.	1⅝	4¼
Essex Chemical Corp.	2½	6⅜
Evans-Aristocrat Industries	4⅛	8⅝
Fab Industries, Inc.	1⅛	3⅞
Fabri-Centers of America	4⅜	14¼
Family Dollar Stores, Inc.	1½	5
Fanny Farmer Candy Shops, Inc.	3⅜ B	9¼
Film Corp. of America	⅝	2⅝
Flight Safety Int'l, Inc.	6¾	15⅜
Fluke (John) Mfg. Co., Inc.	10¼	23⅝
Galaxy Carpet Mills, Inc.	1⅜ B	4⅛
General Housewares Corp.	⁷⁄₁₆	1¼
Gladding Corp.	1¼	2⅝
Globe Industries, Inc.	3½	10¾
Golden West Mobile Homes	1¼ B	5⅜
Good (L S) & Co.	1⅛	2¼
Grand Auto, Inc.	3⅛	6¼
Great Lakes Chemical Corp.	11	28½
Great Lakes Recreation Co.	2⅜ B	5
Greenman Bros, Inc.	¾	2½
Greer Hydraulics, Inc.	2⅜ B	5¼
Guilford Mills, Inc.	2¼	5⅝
Hampton Industries, Inc.	1⅛	3⅝
Harman Int'l Industries	5⅝	16
Hasbro Industries, Inc.	1⅝ B	3½
Health-Chem Corp.	2¼ B	5¾
Highland Capital Corp.	1⅝	3½
House of Ronnie, Inc.	1¾ B	4⅛
Hospitality Motor Inns	3⅝ B	7⅝

Stock	*Lowest sale or bid price Jan. 2, 1975*	*Highest sale or bid price Dec. 31, 1975*
Howell Industries, Inc.	¾ B	3⅜
Hycel, Inc.	2	4
Imperial Chemical Industries, Ltd.	2⅞ B	6⅝ B
Inarco Corp.	1¼	2½
Incoterm Corp.	2	8¾
Inflight Services, Inc.	⅝	1⅝
Intermedco, Inc.	13/16	2½
Int'l Banknote Co., Inc.	5/16	1⅜
Int'l Couriers Corp.	6¾	19¾
Int'l Seaway Trading Corp.	1 B	4¼
Jaclyn, Inc.	3½ B	8⅝
Jamesway Corp.	1¾ B	4¾
Jeanette Corp.	3⅜	8⅜
K Tel Int'l, Inc.	1¼ B	3⅜
Kingstip, Inc.	1¾ B	5
Kleinert's, Inc.	1¼ B	4¼
Knickerbocker Toy Co., Inc.	4⅝	11
Kollmorgen Corp.	7¾	20
Kuhn's Big K Stores Corp.	2½	10
La Pointe Industries, Inc.	2⅜ B	6
Laneco, Inc.	1⅜ B	3⅜
Levitt Industries, Inc. (Formerly Parkway Distributors to August 1975)	2¾	6¾
Liberty Fabrics of N.Y., Inc.	1½ B	6
Lincoln American Corp.	1¼	3¼
Lloyd's Electronics, Inc.	2¼ B	5⅝
MPO Videotronics, Inc.	1 B	2⅜
Marlene Industries Corp.	1⅝	6⅛
Masoneilan Int'l Inc.	5½	23¾
Maul Brothers, Inc.	2	4⅛
McDonough Co.	6	13½
McIntosh Corp.	3¼ B	6⅞
Medenco, Inc.	3⅛	6¼
Mego International, Inc.	2½	10¼
Midland Glass Co., Inc.	4⅛	10⅛
Miller-Wohl Co., Inc.	3 3/16	30⅜
Movielab, Inc.	⅞	1⅞
Napco Industries, Inc.	1¾	3⅞
National Distributing Co.	2½	5¾
National Industries 1978 Warrants	½	1⅛

Stock	Lowest sale or bid price Jan. 2, 1975	Highest sale or bid price Dec. 31, 1975
National Paragon Corp.	2⅞	6
National Systems Corp.	⅜	1⅝
Nationwide Homes, Inc.	5⅛ B	17⅜
New Process Co.	3¾	14⅛
Niagara Frontier Services	5¼	12¾
Nichols (S E), Inc.	⅞ B	2¼
Noel Industries	1	2⅜
Novo Corp.	1¼ B	3¼
Oakwood Homes Corp.	3⅜ B	6⅞
Ohio-Sealy Mattress Mfg.	4¼	10
Olla Industries, Inc.	1⅜	4¼
Originala, Inc.	⅝	1⅞
Oxford First Corp. (Pa.)	1	2¾
P & F Industries, Inc.	¾ B	2⅛
Pandel-Bradford, Inc.	1½	4½
Parsons (Ralph) M. Co.	11	22⅜
Pat Fashions Industries	⅞	2½
Penobscot Shoe Co.	1⅛	2⅝
PepCom Industries, Inc.	4⅛ B	10¾
Pertec Corp.	1⅝	3⅜
Pic'n Pay Stores, Inc.	2⅛	7⅝
Pioneer Texas Corp.	2¼	5⅞
Plant Industries, Inc.	3⅜	8½
Plantronics, Inc.	4	16¼
Pneumo Corp.	4½	11⅞
Poloron Products, Inc.	⁵⁄₁₆	1
Presley Companies	1⅝	5⅞
Ranchers Exploration & Development	7¾	17½
Refrigerated Transport Co.	1¾	3⅞
Research-Cottrell, Inc.	4⅞	13⅞
Resistoflex Corp.	5⅞	13⅞
Riblet Products Corp.	1⅛ B	2⅜
Richton International Corp.	¾	4
Ronco Teleproducts, Inc.	⁹⁄₁₆	1⅜
Ruddick Corp.	1⅜	3
Rusco Industries, Inc.	½	1
STP Corp.	3¼	7⅜
Salem Corp.	3¼	11¼
Sambo's Restaurants, Inc.	7¾	15⅝
Saunders Leasing System	3	6
Scheib (Earl), Inc.	3¼	6⅞

Stock	*Lowest sale or bid price Jan. 2, 1975*	*Highest sale or bid price Dec. 31, 1975*
Scientific-Atlanta, Inc.	4½	11¼
Shearson Hayden Stone, Inc.	2	4⅞
Shelter Resources Corp.	1¹⁄₁₆	2½
Silo, Inc.	1⅝	3¾ B
Sky City Stores, Inc.	3⅛	7⅜
Solitron Devices, Inc.	¹⁵⁄₁₆	2½
Soundesign Corp.	4¾	13
Spencer Companies, Inc.	¹⁵⁄₁₆	3⅜
Standard-Pacific Corp.	1½	3⅛
Standard Products Co.	7¾	15¾
Standard Shares, Inc.	10½	21½
State Savings & Loan Assn.	3½	10⅝
Steelmet, Inc.	3½	8⅙
Sun Electric Corp.	9	19⅜
Superior Industries Int'l, Inc.	1½	4
Systems Engineering Labs	¹⁵⁄₁₆	6⅛
Technical Tape, Inc.	¾	1¾
Tenna Corp.	1	2¼
Tidwell Industries, Inc.	¾	2⅛
Tiffany Industries, Inc.	3¼ B	8⅝
Tokheim Corp.	4⅛	11⅞
Tracor, Inc.	1⅞	4⅞
Trico Industries, Inc.	1 B	4
Tuftco Corp.	1⅜ B	3
Turbodyne Corp.	2⅜	9½
UIP Corporation	1⅜	3
U.S. Filter Corp.	4	8⅝
U.S. Natural Resources	1¾	3⅝
Universal Rundel Corp.	3	6¼
Varo, Inc.	1⅛	4⅞
Vermont American Corp.	5¾	15
Vertipile, Inc.	½ B	1⅛
WUI, Inc.	7⅛ B	15¾
Westates Petroleum Co.	3¾	9¾
Winston Mills, Inc.	⁹⁄₁₆	2⅝
Zimmer Homes Corp.	1¾	4⅝

Two things are worth noting in this tabulation: (1) that as many as 200 issues doubled; and (2) that almost 90 percent of them were selling below $5 on Jaunary 1, 1975. This documents the theory we have developed, namely, that to pick doublers the best market sector to work in is among the mini-shares.

It's difficult to isolate the specific forces that caused each of these stocks to double, but the following observations are pertinent. On the basis of industry, eight were petroleum-oriented, several chemical issues performed well, and there were a number of textiles that reflected a moderate upturn in the last half of 1975. In a single category, mobile homes were most impressive, with Coachmen, Golden West, Nationwide, Oakwood and Zimmer Homes gaining, on the average, over 200 percent, in response to an improved outlook for that industry plus some gains in net profits in the last quarter of the year.

Child World reported no gain in earnings in 1975, but its prospects for 1976 were brightened by the general economic recovery. Miller-Wohl, operating apparel specialty shops, made the best gain, moving from 3⅞ to 30⅜ apparently in response to earnings that advanced from $1.68 in 1974 to $3.08 in 1975. Such upthrust in profits scarcely accounts for so great a rise, however. It is possible that efforts were made somewhere along the line to popularize this issue.

Bergen Brunswig, which ran up from 2¼ to 6¼, seemed to be propelled not only by an earnings gain (24¢ in 1974 to 63¢ in 1975) but a glamour attached to its Health Applications Subsidiary. This division administers third-party prescription programs and applies computer techniques to programs of health care. In fiscal 1975, "HAS" administered over 26 million claims and was awarded a contract for complete administration of North Carolina's Medicaid program, with comparable volume business in the offing. (The stock continued to project a growth image, rising to 17⅜ in April, 1976 but descending thereafter.)

Cablecom and Cox Cable indicated a new hope for cable TV. Gladding was foretelling an increase in leisure time expenditures (fishing and winter sports) plus the rising popularity of Citizen Band radios, produced by a Gladding subsidiary. (GDD common continued its rise, to above 10 in early 1976.)

Jamesway, a self-service discount store, benefited from the rise in consumer spending, and its earnings rose well above the 53¢ a share reported in 1974. Kuhn's Big K Stores (discount department and variety), Dillard Department Stores, Drug Fair, New Process Company, Sambo's Restaurants,

Pic 'n Pay Stores, Knickerbocker Toy (stuffed animals), and Benrus Corporation all documented the rising trend in consumer spending. Coleman Company, makers of camping equipment, showed a sharp upturn in its profits. Earl Scheib, Inc. proved that people would spend more money painting their cars when the economy turned up. Shearson Hayden Stone and A. G. Edwards anticipated the rising volume and profits in stock trading which materialized in 1976. Bowne & Co. was convinced that financial reports and prospectuses were going to be a busy field in the months ahead.

It would not be particularly useful to try to conjecture the cause for gain in each one of the 200 issues. Many shares apparently rose without any special technical or fundamental justification, just because there was greater confidence in the economy, because an election year lay ahead, and because, in certain cases, marginal companies could breathe a sigh of relief after renewing or lengthening their bank loans. They also received some benefit from declining interest rates.

Those shares, however, that showed the greatest gains did so for a particular reason. If we are to succeed in picking future doublers, we must be on the lookout for comparable special features in companies under consideration that can propel their stocks upward. It is important not only to consider the merits of a stock on the basis of its current operations but also to ask ourselves: Has this company a new product? Will it benefit from some new demand (smog or pollution control, electronic home protection, smaller motor cars, denim clothing, tennis shoes, gaudy sports shirts, brush pens, Citizen Band radios, imprinted T-shirts)? Nothing is so likely to make money for you in the market as early anticipation of a powerful market trend. The gains in many of the AMEX issues in 1975 derived, in a major way, from an *anticipation* of trends, some of which we cited.

Seek out these new streams of innovation or expansion, and then research for companies in line to benefit. In this way, you may not get stocks suitable for long-term holding, but you will locate issues with potentials for exciting gains once you identify companies riding toward the crest of a fad or fashion. You may get equally impressive results with a company emerging from the brink of insolvency.

Look once again at Table I to reassure yourself that there exist, in reasonable profusion, stocks on a major exchange that can double in a year. Then resolve to be on the alert for industrial areas likely to expand, and seek out a group of companies to follow. In particular, watch their earnings, as regularly reported in the financial press. At least 20 percent of the shares in Table I were telegraphing their potentials for market gain as they registered increases in net earnings, quarter by quarter.

In the long run, stock prices are the slaves of earning power. An upturn in a stock is most likely to occur as soon as the public is aware that a downtrend in profits has been reversed, or a notable gain in net appears in the latest quarterly statement. These favorable statistics, plus public notice of a breakthrough in any significant area (product, technology, merger, etcetera) are some of the fuels that propel shares upward.

1. Greater confidence in the economy.

2. Election year ahead.

Chapter III

The $2 Window in Wall Street: Spectacular Opportunities in Low-Priced Stocks

When you read an edition of the *Wall Street Journal*, you get sheaves of news about the economy, the big corporations and elite financial institutions, and the trading activity and volume in a hundred or more "sacred cow" top-tier equities. However, these *Wall Street Journal* pages have almost nothing to say about low-priced stocks—those selling at $5 or less. This same vacuum of information about mini-equities exists in most other financial pages and journals. This is unfortunate because exciting action and dramatic price swings occur every day among low-priced stocks. Thousands of bold speculators have made killings by fortunate early purchase of stocks so low-priced that institutional portfolio managers never even heard about them!

The purpose of this book is to correct this situation: to provide more adequate information in this high-risk, high-gain market for those who seek it. We will not underestimate the high risks, but we will try to minimize them by zeroing in on the best of the golden opportunities for remarkable gain lurking among the market long shots at "the $2 Window in Wall Street."

There are now about 28 million active stockholders in America (not including the 80 million more who own stocks unwittingly through their pension funds and insurance policies). Most of the 28 million are primarily interested in seasoned, dividend-paying stocks that afford reasonable expectations for long-term gain. They're not aiming at killings but rather at second incomes and financial serenity in the later, retirement years.

But of this 28 million, 20 percent are speculators, eager for market "action," always scanning the stock tables for go-go stocks selling for "peanuts." These market activists are not impressed when IBM gains 20 points—that's only 10 percent on a $200 stock. They want things like Atlas Warrants, which moved from 50¢ to $3 in six months in 1975, or Kaufman & Board, which went from 3 to 10¼ in even less time.

Because stocks below $5 appear twice as likely to double in a year's time as those selling at $10 or higher, speculators love them. They relish ownership of a sheaf of certificates. They'd much rather have 500 shares at $2 than 50 shares at $20. Also, a small outlay may produce a greater dollar gain in a lucky low-priced stock. In an outstanding speculative year—1967, for example—of 396 issues that doubled (or more) in price on AMEX, 166 started out below $5; and the total gains in percentages were far more spectacular in this group of 166. (Just for the record, the winner in that year was Cameo Parkway, which soared on AMEX from 2¼ to 74, a gain of 3,300 percent!)

There's another point about low-priced stocks that, obvious as it is, should be emphasized, and that is the key matter of potential for gain. As I mentioned previously, if you buy a stock at 100 and it goes up five points, you've made a 5 percent gain. If you buy a stock at 5 and it goes up five points, you've scored a 100 percent gain. Of course, a stock at 100 is more likely to gain five points than one at 5—but not twenty times more likely (especially if you've selected a genuine potential doubler, hopefully with the help of this book). We're addressing ourselves here to *speculators,* and the "$2 (to $5 or $6) Window on Wall Street" gives you your best shot at a killing, large or small—depending on the amount you can *afford* to gamble, the degree of guidance you get from this book, your own acumen, and of course, that patron saint of all speculators, Lady Luck.

And then, of course, there's always the chance that a low-priced stock you originally bought for speculation can evolve into a pillar of the Wall Street Establishment. Indeed, amazing gains and substantial fortunes have been racked up by early buyers and patient holders of dynamic mini-stocks. Xerox, Computing Tabulating and Recording (the forerunner of IBM), Syntex, Coastal States Gas, Tampax, Government Employees Insurance, Jefferson-Pilot Insurance, Houston Oil and Minerals, Walt Disney, Franklin Life—all fortune-builders for their long-term holders—once sold below $5 a share. Control Data sold at 2⅛ in 1958 and reached 156 in 1968!

Needless to say, one musn't get carried away by these figures. The odds are *always* high against duplicating such bonanzas. With guidance, however, the odds naturally improve.

Granted that outstanding opportunities exist at all times in this submerged market sector, and that three generations of men and women with sporting blood have constantly been looking for them, why have low-priced stocks been such pariahs among brokerage firms? Seldom indeed does a substantial brokerage house recommend a stock trading below $5. Most will deliberately discourage investment in, or even inquiry about, shares in this plebeian market range.

Here are some of the formidable roadblocks they set up. Major NYSE firms may present one, several, or all of the following deterrents to trading in low-priced stocks. They may:

(1) Decline to accept (or execute) an unsolicited "buy" order.

(2) Require that the customer state that he or she is buying the stock "on his own" and not relying on any information or recommendation supplied by the firm.

(3) Ban solicitation by customers' brokers of orders in "below $5" issues; or deny commission credit on such orders, if taken and executed.

(4) Not accept an order ($5 or below range) unless it is a "market" order (with no specified price).

(5) Require written memos from customers' brokers citing the basis for soliciting orders in any low-priced shares, whether listed or OTC.

(6) Expect that "our brokers will attempt to discourage clients from buying low-priced or unseasoned stocks" and warn them of the inherent speculative risks.

(7) Provide no margin accommodation on $5 stocks, and reduce or terminate loans in existing margin accounts when issues used as collateral move to below $5.

(8) Execute orders (if at all) only on behalf of old customers.

There is usually, however, no impediment to "sell" orders in such issues, regardless of price, at standard commissions.

The two basic motives in back of all these restrictive measures are: (1) to protect the brokerage firm against the possible claim of a client that, at the insistence of the firm or its representative, he had been persuaded to buy a security of great risk or dubious merit; and (2) to confine brokerage transactions to seasoned securities, seeking greater dollar volume with less paperwork.

Further, research departments of large firms are simply not staffed or equipped to supply adequate information on a myriad of smaller companies. Markets are usually thinner and less active in their shares, and getting a quote on an issue in this sector uses up a trader's time, keeping him from working on larger, more rewarding executions. Further, the details of confirmation, billing, collection, and stock transfer are just as costly and time-consuming for mini-stocks as for larger orders, and generally afford less gross profit. Also, firms that are expanding, and taking on or training new brokers, are hesitant to have these less experienced associates guide clients in the selection of high-risk, low-priced issues.

As a consequence, firms prefer to confine their recommendations, and their customers' purchases, to seasoned securities with broad trading markets, those with extensive statistical material available about them, rather than to get involved in securities of lower price and quality, vulnerable in weak markets and during periods of economic stress, possibly creating liabilities for the house.

All these dissuading restrictions seem a bit curious when the shares of certain well-known NYSE firms have themselves sold not long ago below $5! In 1974, Paine, Webber; A. G. Edwards; Bache; Reynolds Securities; J. H. Oliphant & Co.; and Donaldson, Lufkin and Jenrette all did!

Not only have major brokerage houses discouraged speculative transactions, but the American Stock Exchange has, on occasion, taken its own steps to dampen market speculation that it regarded as dangerous or excessive. In May, 1968, AMEX sent out a letter to several companies whose shares (quoted then at $5 or below) were being heavily traded. It requested that these companies either "reverse split" their shares (so that they would trade in a higher price range) or face the possibility of delisting. As a consequence, on June 17, 1968, AMEX trading in the stocks of four companies was discontinued—Canada Southern, Magellan Petroleum, Pancoastal, Inc., and United Canso Oil and Gas. (They all moved over to the National Stock Exchange.)

Our contention is that the doors to low-priced speculation should be kept open. These are the kinds of securities relished by the smaller speculator. By unduly restrictive procedures, he or she may, indeed, be denied notable profit opportunities for shrewd early acquisition of winners, such as Tampax, Occidental Petroleum, Xerox, or McDonald's—typical rewarding equities that once sold below $5.

EXAMPLES

In the autumn of 1956, Occidental Petroleum was a fledgling enterprise in Los Angeles, with 800,000 shares outstanding, quoted at 18¢ a share. Dr. Armand Hammer, who had earlier made a lot of money selling such diverse commodities as furs, caviar, wheat, pencils, distilled spirits, and art, supplied OXY with some money it needed for oil drilling exploration in return for stock. In 1957, Dr. Hammer became president of OXY and has been its guiding spirit ever since.

By 1963, the company got into the black and stayed there. Fertilizer companies and Jefferson Lake Sulphur were acquired, and, most important, a large drilling concession in Libya was secured, on which OXY drilled some of the most successful wells in the world in a field called Idris-A. Further acquisitions included McWood Corporation, Permian Corporation, Island Creek Coal, and Hooker Chemical. One hundred shares of OXY stock bought at 20¢ in 1956, or $1.25 in 1962, became 300 shares by July, 1968, worth $13,500.

Another stock, awash with glamour, that made fortunes for hundreds of individuals was Control Data Corporation. It became such a market darling that its common stock sold at 169 times earnings in 1967. It became one of the largest makers of transistorized digital computer systems and related peripheral equipment.

Control Data expanded both internally and by acquisition of C-E-I-R Automatic Control Company, and the giant Commercial Credit Company (1967).

You could have bought Control Data common at $2.50 a share in 1958. After 3 for 1 and 3 for 2 splits, the common sold at 156 in 1968. An original 100-share investment costing $250 attained a market value, at the top, of $70,200. Control Data common stock now sells at more modest levels (around 23). But what a winner!

Tampax, McDonald's Corporation, Syntex, and Disney

Productions all sold below $5 at one time, and all have been amazingly rewarding to early buyers. Denial of opportunity for early entry into such explosive stocks may be a costly disservice to speculators with money they can afford to risk.

Going back to the Great Depression, there were dozens of issues you might have bought as such bargain prices with fantastic results! Here are some random quotations from mid-1932:

American Cyanamid	$2
Carrier Corporation	$2.50
Celanese	$1.25
Crum & Foster	$3
Douglas Aircraft (now McDonnell Douglas)	$5
Phillips Petroleum	$2
Parker Pen	$2.50
Cutler Hammer	$3.50
Shell Union Oil (now Shell Oil)	$2.50

Pretty impressive list of companies, isn't it? Well, assume you had invested $1,000 in one or more of these issues at that time, retaining your holdings intact until 1975. Do you realize that *any* of these would have generated a capital gain of 100-fold or more? At the very least, your original $1,000 would have grown to $100,000!

These examples illustrate the truly remarkable profits possible from shares bought for "peanuts." And dozens of other companies have performed comparably.

The point we want to make is that opportunities are always there, even though the individual odds against your buying a market virtuoso are probably something like 200 to 1. Speculating in this sector can challenge your judgment and market perception, add zest to your life—and, with luck, keep you in Cadillacs.

While we have just cited the exciting gains for those who boldly bought star-kissed issues and hung on, there have been dozens of instances where market agility and an intuition to sell were the winning ploys—and not dogged tenacity. Look at some of the famous market yo-yos! Solitron Devices common ranged in the OTC market between 1¼ and 5⅜ in 1962. It was an early virtuoso in solid-state semi-conductors, and its earnings surged upward from 1962 to 1968.

After a 2 for 1 split in 1966, and a 5 for 1 split in 1968, Solitron sold at 36 (8/22/68). A hundred shares at $2 bought in 1962 became 1,020 shares worth $36,000. But the stock has since backed off and sells at around 3.

Lum's, a Florida-based, low-priced specialty restaurant chain, had a lot of early speed. Its shares went from a low of 25¢ in 1964, after a 3 for 1 split, to 47 in the OTC market in 1968—$25 to $14,000 in four years. Then the business moved downhill, and today Lum's common is no glamour stock.

Another roller coaster is Bermac Corporation. It started out as a truck rental company, then moved disastrously into cattle breeding through its acquisition of Black Watch Farms. Bermac common rose from 4⅞ in 1966 to 90½ in 1968. It later dove in price as the Black Angus business turned out to be mostly bull, and customers of the firm found they were buying livestock at grossly inflated prices. Bermac common may fetch around 10¢ today.

Most people recall the sensational gains made by Equity Funding Corporation and National Student Marketing. They later became involved in ghastly losses and litigation. Equity Funding reached 81⅜ and National Student Marketing 71½ in 1967–68. Those individuals who had racked up dizzy paper profits in these comets saw their market values vanish as cosmetic accounting and serious irregularities came to light. There are surely enough risks in putting money in low-priced stocks without having to cope with unethical management as well!

The vicissitudes of the market are sufficient to produce disheartening downswings, even in the securities of considerable merit. All listed stocks, in the aggregate, shed 70 percent of their market values between 1966 highs and 1974 lows. Within this period, Addressograph Multigraph dove from a high of 91 to a low of 3¾; Talley Industries from 65 to 5; Technicolor from 45 to 5; Penn Central from 86½ to 1; United Brands from 58⅜ to 2⅜; Winnebago from 48¼ to 3; Levitz Furniture from 60½ to 1¼; Monogram Industries from 81¾ to 4. These issues are all listed on the NYSE. The price declines on AMEX and in the OTC market in the same period were quite as shattering and far more numerous.

These random selections serve to illustrate that market profits can be ephemeral and elusive; that gainful speculation calls for market agility and timing intuition (a little inside information can help); and that some highly respected equities can descend quite suddenly to the "$2 Window." While these declines represent tragedy for thousands, the same stocks may become golden buying opportunities after they have reached bottom.

It is obvious that this whole business of trading in mini-stocks can be enormously risky but can also prove highly profitable. There is no sure system or formula. Continued retention of a "growth" stock, bought early—such as Disney, IBM, American Home Products, or Pfizer—was the right thing, wheareas speculative darlings—such as Winnebago or Levitz—should have been sold when earnings peaked, in order to keep paper profits from melting like butter in the noonday sun. When or whether to sell are almost as important decisions as when to buy.

As guidance, it might be generally observed that you need not consider the sale of a stock as long as its earnings remain in a vigorous, uninterrupted upcurve. When sales and profits show signs of significant slippage, a sale should probably be considered, unless the decline can be accounted for by a special condition, such as a fire, a strike, an earthquake, or an Arab oil ripoff, or a national emergency, such as war, invasion, or epidemic.

Many speculators follow a formula that offers an arbitrary solution to the problem of "when to sell." It is called "Operation Bait Back." When you buy a low-priced stock, sell half of it, if and when it has gained 200 percent. You buy, say, 1,000 shares of Zilchboom Electronics at 2, spending $2,000. If it advances to 6, sell half (500 shares) realizing $3,000. Out of this $3,000, you can defray the capital gains tax, your round-trip commissions, and transfer taxes. That will return your $2,000 stake with a tidy clear profit and, best of all, you will own the other half (the 500 shares you keep) "free and clear" and can blithely delay, indefinitely, any further decision about its sale. Regardless of circumstances, you have profitably insured against a yo-yo downspin in the issue and have retained 500 "free" shares in case of an upturn. If the stock later rises to $20 and you sell for $10,000, you're miles ahead. After "Operation Bait Back," you're always a winner! Of course, for this to work, the stock has to triple, but this happens often enough in low-priced stocks to make it a reasonable possibility.

We have now provided sufficient background in citing past market opportunities and dazzling gains, and dismal price descents into the market cellar. This is the area that provides action, zest and high expectations—along with dashed hopes. For those reasonably diligent in research (and blessed with luck), possessed of surplus funds they can afford to lose, and capable of accepting dramatic swings in the market, up or down, with equanimity, there are opportunities galore—literally thousands of stocks from which to select.

SCOPE OF THE LOW-PRICED SHARE MARKET

Of the 40,000 different issues of common stocks that are traded on NYSE, AMEX, the regional exchanges, Over-the-Counter, and in Canadian markets, over 25 percent sold at $5 or less on August 2, 1975. Probably no more than 7,000 out of this 40,000 are traded in sufficient daily volume to be quoted in the newspapers. The "pink" trading sheets, used by brokerage professionals, are published daily by National Quotation Bureau and list the bid and asked prices of several thousand more. Hundreds of these are small issues of local or regional companies, publicly offered and distributed during the "going public" mania of the 1960's by underwriting firms no longer in business. Others in this large group are the equities of marginal and struggling corporations that manage to survive but not really to succeed—in mining, manufacturing, marketing, energy, real estate, scientific, or service industries.

The largest single category among very low-priced stocks is mining. Both in Canada and the United States, thousands of small companies have sold shares to the public and have planned to explore for, and to mine, gold, silver, copper, lead, zinc, nickel, etcetera. Most of these have bales of shares outstanding and are as deficient in capital as in ore bodies, with thin or nonexistent share markets, and trading, if at all, in pennies. The largest catalog of such mining companies is found in the Canadian Mines Handbook, published annually.

Dozens of lowly stocks, however, are those of substantial and well-known companies that have plummeted into the market cellar from more exalted price levels of better days. Of these, Penn Central is the classic example.

The denizens of the low-priced sector change each day, as some graduate, some disappear, and some others enter. At the bottom of the 1974 market decline, there were probably more issues selling below $5 than at any other time in history. (There were, of course, many stocks selling in that range in 1932–33 but their total number at that time was far lower because thousands of companies have "gone public" since.)

In a representative market day, selected entirely at random—August 19, 1975—out of 1,778 issues traded on NYSE, some 165 sold at $5 or below; and of 856 traded that day on AMEX, 404 sold at $5 or below. On the OTC market, there were thousands more. There's obviously an ample shopping list here with sufficient diversity to suit every purse and taste. The only problem is how to winnow the winners from the losers.

Regardless of the time of your entry into this bargain basement, there are certain things you should know about issues you are considering. You must develop satisfactory evidence that the company in which you risk your dollars has: (1) the essential ingredients for survival; (2) some potential for rising profits and possible dividends; (3) the capability of attracting market sponsorship and an animated market following. Stocks do not go up unless there are more buyers than sellers! Indeed, many issues rise spectacularly without any persuasive statistical justification, simply because they have become popular and get talked about in metropolitan board rooms. Sudden market enthusiasm, sparking strong price uptrends, is often based on nothing more than rumor: of a new offshore oil strike; of an exciting new patent, process, or pharmaceutical product; of a possible acquisition or merger; of entry into a new product or service field; of displacement of a weak and weary management with a capable new group. Anything that smacks of romance, glamour, or new horizons of profitability, or injects flickers of hope into some forlorn company, may cause a low-priced stock to advance madly when avid traders and speculators "get the message."

Therefore, in your quest for rewarding mini-stocks, make allowance for this unknown, mystical or rumor element. Remember, also, that there are fad enthusiasms for some favorite industry from time to time. Riding the tide of market fashion can often reward a trader more richly and swiftly than buying an issue on the basis of a good balance sheet and a defined earnings' uptrend in an unglamorous industry, providing one knows when to get off the merry-go-round. Remember how baby uranium shares soared in 1954?

There were 400 new offerings of uranium stocks that year, many gaining 200 to 500 percent within a few months. Where are they today? Mostly out of business. Only a dozen or so lived, or merged, to become significant and successful enterprises.

In 1961, bowling was erroneously assumed to be the coming major pastime of mankind. The "biggies" were American Machine & Foundry and Brunswick. The latter soared to 74⅞ in 1961—and sank to 6 in 1966. A couple dozen bowling alley chains publicly offered their stocks around the $5 level, and two quite sizable satellite companies emerged, Bowl-Mor (pinsetters) and Bar-Cris (alley builders). Both zoomed in 1961–62, and both later went bankrupt!

In 1967, computer and leasing stocks were the market darlings. In 1968, fried chicken, hamburger chains, and nursing homes were all the rage; in 1970 it was the REITs; in 1972–73 it was oil shares and golds. And so it goes—every year or two, a new favorite industry emerges with large volume trading of shares, almost always followed by a later agonizing descent from a madly inflated price level. Few stocks indeed ever merit a P/E multiple above 40 over any length of time; above that ratio, they are almost invariably "a sale," meaning, sell now—or else!

Accordingly, temper your hopes and dreams of killings in mini-shares with the realization that market popularity is a capricious thing. Be prepared to jump nimbly out before your modish stock goes out of style, or you may be left holding a "cluck." In the stock market, "Nothing recedes like excess!"

To illustrate the panorama of opportunities in stocks at $5 or below, we have assembled the following tables. Table II is a complete list of such issues on NYSE at a given period; Table III gives incomplete and random selections from AMEX; and Table IV provides selections from the OTC market.

P/E 40 = SELL

TABLE II

Stocks on the New York Stock Exchange
Trading at or below $5
Week of April 5, 1976

Company	Quotation
Adams Drug	4
AJ Industries (P)	2⅞
Allied Supermarkets	4⅜
American Century Mtg.	1¾
American Finance System	3¼
American Investment	4
Amrep Corp.	2⅜
Apeco Corp. (P)	2¾
Applied Magnetics (P)	3¾
Arctic Enterprises (P)	5
Aristar	2⅞
Arlen Realty & Dev.	3½
Armada Corp. (P)	5
Atico Mtg.	2¾
Atlas Corp. (P)	4⅞
Beneficial Standard Mtg.	2½
Benguet B (P)	2⅛
Berkey Photo	4½
Borman's (P)	4
BT Mortgage Inv.	2⅝
Cabot Cabot & Forbes	2¾
Cadence Indus.	4¼
Caesars World	3⅞
Cameron Brown	2⅝
Capital Mtg.	1¾
Carling O'Keefe Ltd.	3⅞
CCI Corp.	2⅜
Charter (P)	4⅛
Chase Manhattan Mtg. Realty	3⅛
Chock Full O'Nuts	3¼
CI Realty Inv.	3½
Citizens & Southern Realty	2¾
CLC of America	5¼
Cook United (P)	4⅞
Cordura Corp.	1¾
Cousins Mtg.	2½
Credithrift Financial (P)	4¼
Deltec Intl (P)	4
Diversified Mtg. Inv.	1⅞
Duplan	4

Electronic Assoc. (P)	4
Electronic Mem. & Mag.	3
EMI Ltd. (P)	5
Fidelity Financial (P)	4⅞
First Penna Mtg.	2⅝
First Virginia Bank	5¾
General Steel Indus. (P)	5
Grolier	2⅝
Guardian Mtg. Inv.	2⅛
Gulf Mtg. & Realty	2½
ICN Pharmaceuticals	5
Institutional Investor Trust	1⅝
Ipco Hospital Supply	5
Justice Mtg.	3
Katy Indus. (P)	4⅛
Lehigh Valley Indus.	1½
LFE Corp. (P)	4⅝
Liberty Loan	3⅜
Lionel Corp. (P)	3¾
EF MacDonald (P)	4⅝
Madison Square Garden (P)	5¾
JW Mays	5⅜
MEI Corp.	4⅞
Midland Mtg. Inv.	1⅞
Morse Electro. Prod.	3
Mortgage Trust of Amer.	3⅛
National Tea	4¾
North Central Airlines (P)	3⅝
Northgate Explorations (P)	5
Penn Central	1⅞
Planning Research (P)	3¾
Playboy Enterprises (P)	4
Publicker Indus. (P)	4⅝
Pueblo Intl.	3¼
Puerto Rican Cement	4½
Puritan Fashions (P)	5⅞
Republic Mortgage Inv.	1⅞
Rexham Corp. (P)	5⅝
Ronson Corp.	5¼
Safeguard Indus. (P)	4
Saul REIT	3⅝
Sav-A-Stop	5¼
SCA Services	3⅛
F & M Schaefer	5
Seaboard World Air (P)	4¾
Seatrain Lines	4⅝
Sonesta Intl. (P)	4½
State Mutual Inv.	1¾

Suave Shoe (P)	5
Sutro Mtg.	4⅞
Talcott National	4⅛
Telex (P)	4¼
UMET Trust	1¾
Union Fidelity (P)	4¾
United Park City Mine	2⅛
U.S. Realty Inv.	2⅛
Wachovia Realty	3⅝
Wyly Corp.	4⅞

(P) denotes that the stock reported net earnings (even though sometimes only a few pennies per share) in the latest 12-month figures reported by the company, prior to April 1, 1976. The others reported current losses.

Table II was prepared to establish that, even on the most elite security exchange in the world, there are plenty of stocks selling below $5—actually, 97 in the week we selected. Thus in spring, 1976, your selection from cellar stocks could have begun with roughly 100 trading at $5 or below on NYSE, followed by over 300 on AMEX and several thousand in the OTC market. Such a large catalog of issues establishes the point we've been trying to make: that customary practices in the securities industry and among leading broker/dealers discriminate against by virtually excluding reference to, or research and quotation services on, thousands of issues. Why? Because these issues may be too small, too low-priced or too inactive to pay off—for the broker.

Even the list of shares in Table II represents practically the dregs of the issues listed on NYSE. You'll note that only a third of the issues were showing any sort of net profits. The largest category on the list was 21 REITs, all operating at a loss in the preceding twelve months. The winner in this negative sweepstake was Guardian Mortgage Investors, which reported a loss of $26.95 a share in the latest 12-month period covered prior to April, 1976. Obviously a selection from this $5 group on NYSE requires that you probe for information about when these unprofitable companies may turn around, or if their common stock will retain any sort of value. One arbitrary way of investing in this list would be to confine your selection to issues still in the black. For further coverage of issues in Table II, you are referred to chapter VI, devoted entirely to REITs and the art of gleaning possible winners from this quite submerged group.

TABLE III

*Random Selection of Low-Priced Shares
On American Stock Exchange*

Issue	3/25/76 Closing Price
Alaska Airlines	5¼
American Motor Inns	5¼
Arrow Electronics	4½
Bluebird, Inc.	4½
California Life	4⅝
Curtis Mathis	3¾
Damson Oil	4½
Eagle Clothing	1⅞
Federal Resources	5
Forest Labs	3⅜
Frontier Air	3
General Builders	1⅜
Inflight Service	2¼
International Funeral	2⅜
Lake Shore Mines	2½
Manhattan Life	4⅝
National System	3⅛
Phoenix Steel	3¾
Rossmoor Corp.	3⅜
Solitron	3¾
Stevco Knit	5⅛
Treadway	4⅛
Wrather Co.	5⅛

TABLE IV

*Random Selections of
Over-the-Counter Stocks*

Issue	9/4/75 Closing Offering Price
Alaska Gold	4½
Agnico-Eagle	5
American Furniture	3⅜
Arvida Corp.	5
Beneficial Standard A	3¾
Clinton Oil	2¼
De Beers	4
Falstaff Brewing	3
Fidelity Corp.	1⅝

Guardian Chemical	2¾
Hyatt Corp.	5
Illinois Beef Packers	4¼
F. L. Jacobs	1½
Keystone Custodian Funds, A	3⅝
Life Investors	5
J. B. Lippincott	4⅞
Magma Power	4
Microwave Associates	3⅝
Motor Club of America	4¾
Massachusetts General Life	4⅛
National Life of Florida	3⅜
National Shoe	4
Oil Shale Corp.	4⅜
Penn Yan Express	4¼
Patent Management	5
Republic National Life	4¼
Scan Data	2⅛
Scotts Inns of America	1⅝
Southern Airways	3½
Texas First Mortgage	1⅝
Travelodge International	4⅜
Triton Oil & Gas	2⅝
U. S. Banknote	4½
Universal Telephone	2½
Vance Sanders	3⅛
Vitramon	2⅞
Van Wyck International	3
Waste Resources	3⅜
Welsbach Co.	3¼
Zenith United Corporation	2⅛

The preceding lists of cellar-dwelling securities were selected at random (a full tabulation would have taken up too many pages). They are presented without even a whisper of endorsement or recommendation. Some of these shares might soar, and some will sink dismally—possibly out of sight. With regard to stocks in this market sector, whether the security is listed or OTC, there are simply no authoritative experts or sophisticated guidelines available for confident selection of ultimate winners. At the least, you should get the latest annual report of the company, or contact a regional firm trading the stock for information about it.

We know a dreamy speculator who, in mid-1974, purchased at random and without any security analysis, twenty different issues on AMEX with only one criterion—they had to be selling below 4 when he bought them. By this quite absurd procedure, his holdings (I have been informed) increased over 150 percent between mid-1974 and March, 1976.

One way to approach the problem of winnowing winners from the market's basement would be to select, say, twenty of the issues most actively traded in a given week. (The volume of trading in each issue appears in the daily stock tables.) Volume (especially at rising prices) is one index of speculative interest. Then get from a current security manual a comparison of sales and net income over the past twelve months, or a report sheet (Dun & Bradstreet, Standard & Poor's, Moody's, Value Line) and learn about the companies that interest you—what they make, profit history, and also net market range of the stock for the past year. Look for any news item that would suggest rising profitability or possible buying for merger purposes. Talk to company officials and get their latest quarterly reports. From this basic research you should be able to eliminate "weak sisters" and locate those with superior prospects. Don't buy just one. Acquire hostages to fortune by purchasing five different issues.

In combing the market for stocks that may turn out to be rewarding performers, you need not be rigidly arbitrary about considering only those at $5 or less. For example, on the same day that the above lists were drawn up, there were a lot of interesting stocks just a bit higher, in the $6 range: Avco, Bache, Chriscraft, and others. If they appeal to you, why shun them just for a dollar or so?

TABLE V

Stocks Selling Below $5
On the New York Stock Exchange
Possibly Worth Investigating

Issue	May 7, 1976 Price
Gulton Industries	5⅛
American Century Mortgage	1½
Penn Dixie	5
Arlen Realty	3¾
Atlas Corp.	5
BT Mortgage Inv.	2½
Grolier	2½
Publicker Industries	4¼
Sonesta International	3⅞

On the American Stock Exchange

Aiken Industries	4
Alaska Airlines	4⅞
American Motor Inns	4⅝
California Life	4⅝
Canadian Export Ins.	4⅛
Federal Resources	4¾
International Funeral	2⅛
Pratt Read	4⅝
Solitron	3⅞
Tenneco Warrants	5⅛

Finally, get to read the technical charts on active stocks. These give you clues not to earning power but to the extent of market interest and popular following of an issue. A fashionable stock may perform brilliantly, unblessed by any particular investment merit, just because it's an "in" stock. Buying by "the herd instinct" may alone be sufficient to make your stock double. Charts help you to see where the herd is running.

The reason for combing over the list of low-priced stocks is that (1) most of the stocks that double next year will come from issues in this range; (2) as you devote time and effort in investigating these cellar-dwellers, you may improve in your judgment and your timing so that, month by month, you may identify a higher percentage of winners.

In later chapters we will present some specific suggestions of issues that may double, many of them in the price range we have been discussing. To whet your appetite, however, we are citing below some possible candidates (all below $5 as this was written). It's a sample list that lends itself to some homework on your part—following the quotations, looking for quarterly earnings, and possibly examining charts on issues that interest you.

Chapter IV

Mining Stocks

For exciting action, dizzy price swings, swift killings as well as dismal downswings, no sector of the stock market beats the mining list! There are literally thousands of issues to choose from, ranging from penny Canadian shares to sleek blue chips, such as Newmont, AMAX, or Noranda. You can buy seasoned issues with long dividend records, or latch onto a "wild one," such as Poseidon, an Australian nickel "spec" that went from 50¢ to $50 in 1971.

Next to agriculture, mining is the world's oldest industry. Beginning around 6,000 B.C., copper was probably the first metal to be mined by man and worked into useful utensils. Next on the metal horizon came gold and silver, attractive and alluring because of their luster, malleability, durability, divisibility, imperviousness to wear and to the elements—and, above all, their scarcity, which continues to this day.

Both metals, since their discovery, have been eagerly sought by the rich and ruling classes as stores of wealth, cherished possessions, and status symbols. They have been deftly crafted into bracelets, earrings, necklaces, bowls, cups, and tiaras. Among Babylonians and Egyptians these metals were worked into adornments for the graves of the departed.

When merchants advanced in their trading beyond the barter stage, they turned to these same metals as media of exchange. In 560 B.C., coinage of silver and gold was invented. Round coins were later minted in uniform sizes, shapes, and weights, and often imprinted with the emblem or face of a king or emperor. This assured genuineness of the currency and made it acceptable in commerce as a useful common denominator for the exchange of goods and services.

GOLD AND SILVER

The gold mines of ancient Nubia, operated by Pharaohs of Egypt, were the forerunners of the fabulously rich mines of South Africa today, spread in a great arc around the city of Johannesburg, and turning out 27 million ounces of gold a year. The silver mines of Spain, which brought riches to Julius Caesar while he was on military duty there, are still productive.

There persists among peoples in almost every land a respect and a desire for gold and silver unabated by the passage of centuries. The search for rich ore bodies and for fortune-building mining ventures is just as popular as ever. The principal difference is that mining now is far more scientific, and miners (in North America) get $300 a week instead of working as slaves, as they did in the times of Queen Nefertiti or Augustus Caesar.

Gold and silver mines. While gold and silver are less important industrially than copper, lead, and zinc, investment interest in these precious metals has accelerated in the past four years, stimulated by phemomenal price rises. Gold moved up to a high of $197.50 an ounce (from $35) and silver to $6.70 (from $1.29). Even though both metals descended in price in 1975–76, investors have not lost interest in them. Both have been regarded for centuries as effective hedges against inflation. Many economists expect a return to double-digit inflation in 1977, in view of our continued huge government deficits—a total of over $150 billion over the past three years.

Accordingly, in view of the sharp decline in gold and in gold shares in 1975, we believe there exist splendid opportunities among these depressed gold mining stocks. We propose to outline in this chapter (1) some useful criteria for the appraisal of gold and silver mines, and (2) some specific issues that appear to have above-average potentials for significant gain.

Gold shares. The "golds" are divided into two groups: the South African companies (accounting for 70 percent of Free World production), and those elsewhere, mostly in North America. Since the South Africans are more important, we'll discuss them first.

About 35 percent of all the gold ever mined has been

produced in South Africa. Here, the ore is found in conglomerate (made up of pebbles and low-grade ore structure) shot through with small particles of gold in "reefs."
These reefs are mineralized bands that may range in thick-
ness from a fraction of an inch up to 90 feet. These reefs
extend in a great arc of several hundred square miles around
the city of Johannesburg, bending south into the Orange
Free State. Some of the mines are enormous. They may
cost over $30 million, have shafts almost two miles deep,
and use air conditioning systems large enough to service the
Empire State Building.

The South African mining industry is controlled by seven
large mining finance houses: Rand Mines, Gold Fields of
South Africa, Consolidated Investment, General Mining &
Finance, Union Corporation, Anglo-South African and An-
glo-Transvaal Consolidated Investment. Each of these is a
major investor in, and operates, a group of mines, supplying
geological and engineering capability, financial resources, and
guidance. All gold produced is purchased and marketed by
the South African Reserve Bank.

Shares of both finance and operating companies are designated in Rands, but American investors generally trade in
American Depository Receipts, issued by trust companies in
the United States, against the actual shares of the subject
companies deposited in their vaults. These receipts, called
ADR's, are regularly traded in the American OTC market.

There are some 39 different issues of publicly held South
African mines. Quite frankly, all of them might double or
more, if gold returned from $115 (as this was written) to the
1974 high of $197.50. However, we have selected from the
group issues that we think would respond with the greatest
animation to any resurgence of inflation around the world,
or any significant jump in the price of gold. Here, as elsewhere, in our selections we are frankly speculative, and we
are giving preference to shares in the lower price ranges.

RANDFONTEIN ESTATES GOLD MINING COMPANY. This
company is one of our top selections for growth and gain
in 1976–77. It is in the Johannesburg Consolidated Group
located in the West Rand. It's a big producer of gold,
and the largest South African mine in uranium as well,
thus poised to benefit from rising prices in either, or
both, minerals. Randfontein is favored because it is a
low-cost mine (about $45 an ounce), has a relatively

small number of shares outstanding (5,413,553), has an estimated life of fifteen years, and is in line for the start of dividend payments in 1976. With American Depository Receipts selling at 18 (as this was written), a move to 36 would not seem implausible, assuming a runup in the gold price to $160 an ounce or higher. Its low cost of production gives Randfontein a lot more stability than marginal mines, and a large recent capital investment (about $60 million) in the Cooke Section property insulates the property from tax or lease payments for some time to come.

HARMONY is a lower-priced mine (2¾), a member of the Rand Mines group located in Orange Free State. It has an indicated life of about 16 years and a current cost of approximately $99 per ounce. There's also considerable uranium tonnage. The existence of 26,884,-650 common shares assures a broad trading market and good daily volume. Further, Harmony is less dependent on importation of labor from Mozambique than other South African mines. Its dividend payout of 83¢ a share in 1975 is attractive, considering that the stock sells currently at 2¾, and provides some additional inducement to speculators. (Most buyers in this range, however, set little store on dividends.) Given the appropriate blend of political stability, and higher gold prices, Harmony might well be attuned to your goal, and could double to $6.

SOUTHVAAL GOLD MINING LTD. is regarded by many metal analysts as among the most attractive on the entire South African list. It's in the Klerksdorp Field and shepherded by Anglo-American. Southvaal has been steadily expanding its ore reserves and grades have been rising. Indicated mine life is 25 years. Future earnings are brightened by large uranium reserves. The price of uranium has been moving up in recent months, and a figure of $35 a pound in 1976 has been conjectured. The high oil prices, and failure to bring into production any substantial new oil or coal properties in 1975, point to an increasing world demand for uranium. Southvaal shares at around $4 offer prospects of higher dividends in 1976 and an increased market following as the elements of long term merit in these shares become more widely known. There are 26 million shares outstanding.

LESLIE GOLD MINES, LTD. is among the "way out" speculations in South Africa you might list, if only for its price range—from a high of 5½ in 1974 to 55¢ as this was written. It paid a 45¢ dividend in 1975—almost its market price. Leslie is a shortlife (5 to 7 years) mine and a highly leveraged speculation on the gold price. There are 16 million shares of Leslie outstanding, and the property is under the able guidance of Union Corporation.

ANGLO-AMERICAN CORPORATION OF SOUTH AFRICA is another we regard with special favor as speculation shares of a mine finance company. This is one of the world-renowned mining organizations controlling an impressive group of companies with combined total assets of over $7 billion. Its own investment portfolio had a market valuation of approximately $1.1 billion at 3/15/76. Its net income after taxes (Rands, converted into dollars) was $97.4 million in 1975, up from $87 million in 1974. The 1975 dividend was 38¢ a share.

The gold properties of Anglo-American are among the leaders of South Africa and include Western Holdings, Welkom, Vaal Reefs, Southvaal, President Brand. If the price of gold should move back up to around $200 an ounce, these properties could zoom and generate a substantial rise in dividend flow to the holding company. While gold is most important, Anglo-American derives around 15 percent of its income from industrial investments, and 20 percent from diamonds. Platinum and copper incomes, also significant, were lower in 1975 due to depressed prices for these metals.

There are 131,369,000 shares of outstanding ANGLY (trading symbol for the American Depository Receipts). The issue is actively traded in Johannesburg, London and OTC in the United States. Price range in 1974–76 was 3⅛ to 9.

The risk that concerns most people about South African investment—gold or anything else—is political. Will South Africa become embroiled with its own blacks? Will it have to rescue Rhodesia? Will Russo-Cuban military and political infiltration lead to border skirmishes and possible Communist invasion of Southwest Africa?

In our view, none of these adverse conditions is likely. South Africa has one of the stablest governments on that continent, and one of the most dynamic economies. While blacks are still mistreated, both wage and living conditions are improving for them. Further, South Africa gives employment to some 360,000 natives of adjoining countries (Botswana, Mozambique, etcetera), and they make far more money in South Africa than they can in their own nations. We see no serious trouble in South Africa for at least another decade. Meanwhile, rich gold mines, rising dividends, and inflated currencies create investment opportunities. The immediate "drags" on South African gold shares are (1) a higher income tax rate, effective in 1976, (2) the rise in South African military budget, which means that the gold will probably have to be sold as produced to supply current funds (and not stockpiled to await higher prices), and (3) racial turmoil.

Elsewhere in the world, substantial gold mines are neither so rich nor so numerous. We have no accurate records of total annual production in Communist nations (principally Russia), but for 1975 it was estimated at approximately 7.3 million ounces. In the Free World, outside South Africa, the major producers are Canada, the United States, Australia, and South America. Of these, Canada is by far the most important, producing 1.6 million ounces in 1975. Total gold production in 1975 was 47 million ounces.

Canadian gold mines. In Canada, the gold mining industry has been slowly phasing out. In 1940, Canada produced 5,310,000 ounces, down by two-thirds in 1975. In 1941, there were 144 Canadian gold mines in operation; today there are only 26, and a number of these are running out of ore. Even the much higher gold prices prevailing since 1972, and the long-range Canadian program of subsidizing marginal gold mines, have not been able to revitalize the industry or to bring significant new mines into production. The only newcomer of stature is the Eagle mine in Joutel, Quebec, which came on stream in late 1974, and now delivers over 80,000 ounces of gold a year.

The largest and richest gold property in Canada is Campbell Red Lake Mines, Ltd. It has an extensive ore body with tons of proven reserves. Ore grade is the highest in Canada, running about 7/10th ounces to the ton. If you are to own only one Canadian gold stock, CRK is the one, both as a long-term dividend payer and a volatile speculation in coming months. It would appear possible that CRK (NYSE trading symbol for the common stock) could advance from 19 currently to double that before the end of 1977. CRK paid an 82½¢ dividend (Canadian funds) in 1975. The stock sold as high as 48⅞ in 1974. Dome Mines, Ltd. (also listed on NYSE) owns 57% of Campbell Red Lake common.

A second Canadian candidate for superior market performance is Agnico-Eagle, formed in 1972 by a merger of Eagle Gold Mines Ltd. and Agnico Mines Ltd., a silver producer in the legendary cobalt silver camp in Ontario. The Eagle property represents a total investment of over $20 million. This facility is a model of streamlined efficiency. So automated is its milling operation that six technicians can keep it in smooth daily operation.

Agnico-Eagle is unique. It is the only sizable publicly owned company in North America devoted exclusively to gold and silver production. Yearly output on the order of 80,000-plus ounces of gold and a million ounces of silver creates the kind of earning power that can enhance rapidly in the event of rising prices for precious metals. In 1974, two producing silver properties were added. Exploration at lower depths of claims adjacent to the present Eagle mine have disclosed additional reserves of good quality ore; these will significantly extend the life of the Eagle Mine. Reported proven, probable and possible reserves at the 1975 year end were 3,151,657 tons, averaging .29 ounces to the ton.

There are 13,862,000 shares of Agnico-Eagle outstanding, listed on the Toronto Stock Exchange and also traded on the OTC in the United States, and held by over 20,000 share owners. Agnico-Eagle has sold as high as $12. From a current quote of 3½ it could repeat and also start paying dividends in 1977.

Other favored Canadians that rise and fall with the gold price are Giant Yellowknife and Camflo, with Yellowknife a better candidate for doubling. If you have plenty of sporting blood, then there's Dumagami, a long-shot, far-out entry that probably needs $200 gold to become profitable. This issue was modestly quoted at 40¢ in April, 1976.

Among United States mines, the popular leader is Homestake, turning out approximately one-third of annual American gold production at its fabulous mine in Lead, South Dakota. Homestake is also a silver producer, has a rich store of uranium ore, and has sizable lead-zinc production in Missouri. Homestake controls over 100,000 prime mineral acres in South Dakota and Wyoming, of which only a small percentage has been classified in mining leases.

Homestake is an active stock, sensitively responsive to any change in the price of gold, or increase in the rate of inflation. While in a higher price range than we generally favor for superior speculative performance, the stock is capable of doubling in the inflationary economy we envision for 1977. There are 11,336,000 common shares outstanding, selling currently at 31½ on NYSE and trading under the symbol HM.

Among other United States gold shares, we find few with really good performance prospects, although there are dozens of small public companies traded OTC or on the Spokane Exchange. Most of these have meager or tired ore bodies and high operating costs. Possibly Alaska Gold, a placer mine, at around 5 (Pacific Exchange) might deserve investigation. Besides Homestake, other large producers are (1) Kennecott Copper which produces about 300,000 ounces a year as a by-product of its copper mine at Bingham Canyon, Utah, and (2) the Carlin Mine of Newmont Mining, with about 200,000 ounces of annual production ahead. The major mine of Golden Cycle in Colorado is being developed under a contract with Texasgulf. Golden Cycle has a 20 percent carried interest, which may be increased if GC helps finance the cost of a new mill.

Of the small long-shot "specs," Klondex Mines, Ltd. (Vancouver) at 30¢ might move, but get an annual report and reliable current information on this—or any other ministock—before you lay out a nickel.

We are not very excited about Australian or South American gold shares. In addition to the risks inherent in all mining issues, investing in foreign countries has the added hazards of political uncertainty, heavy taxation or outright property confiscation, not to mention the possible embargo on repatriation of profits. Western Mining is a low-priced Australian stock that is possibly worth researching, and Pato Consolidated (PO) on AMEX is a seasoned company dredging gold from riverbeds in Colombia. Rosario Resources

(ROS) on NYSE has a very rich gold/silver mine called Pueblo Viejo in the Dominican Republic, but the government there has been negotiating for a higher share of "the take."

Potentially winning gold issues outside of South Africa are not numerous. If the bullion price rises dramatically, however, or we get double-digit inflation in the United States again in 1977, any of the issues we have cited could zoom. They are really not investments in the ordinary sense but rather long-term bets on the price of gold.

Silver mines. Many informed economists and mining men believe that a substantial rise in silver in 1976–77 is more certainly predictable than for gold. If so, then surely one or two of the speculative stocks selected for our "swinging" portfolio should be silver mines.

Here's the rationale. Whereas Treasury officials and Keynsian economists have been bad-mouthing gold and conspiring against it continuously since 1934, silver has no enemies. It's a cherished personal asset, whether in coin, bar, bracelet, necklace, ring, or pitcher. Its industrial uses alone have outpaced the annual production of newly mined silver in each of the past twenty years. Silver is a precious metal universally desired and valued. In India, silver jewelry represents the equivalent of a savings bank account or life insurance policy. Silver coins have been in global circulation for 2,600 years. Silver is widely favored for ornamentation of all kinds and for tableware in the dining rooms of the civilized world.

Technological advances in photography and electronics have expanded rapidly in the past thirty years. Most of these industrial applications use up and destroy silver, whereas 90 percent of all the gold ever surfaced is still around and in use today. New uses are researched for silver each year. Private mints now turn out and market silver memorial pieces, souvenirs, and medallions at an incredible rate. The leader of these, Franklin Mint, is now believed to be the second largest United States user of silver (after Eastman Kodak). Possibly the sophisticated reflectors designed to convert solar rays into energy will create another important demand for silver.

Silver is the best-known conductor of electricity, and it is so durable that it is preferred in the assembly of quality electronic units. In photography, while total volume of consumption is great, the amount of silver in each snapshot film is so small that silver is employed without regard to price. About 50 percent of all silver used industrially in the United States is consumed in electrical and photographic applications.

The non-Communist world used 390 million ounces of silver in 1975, down about 14 percent from total consumption a year earlier. To meet this demand, 235 million ounces of new silver were mined, and the balance supplied by above ground stores from salvage, melted coins, privately held bullion, and exports from India and Pakistan. As these surface stores are used up, year after year, and because our government no longer has huge stockpiles to liquidate, it seems certain that the price of silver is now in a long-term upswing. No new mining production on the horizon seems at all likely to overcome the annual shortfall, which has occurred for twenty years in a row.

The search for desirable silver stocks is not as easy as for gold. Whereas some gold is produced as a by-product of the mining of other metals, most comes specifically from gold mines. Pure silver mines, however, are relatively rare, and over 70 percent of annual silver production is now derived secondarily from mining for lead, zinc, and copper. For example, ASARCO, the fifth largest copper producer and a major producer in lead and zinc, is the largest United States silver producer (7.5 million ounces in 1974). While ASARCO, Inc. common (AR on NYSE, 26,801,000 shares outstanding) is not our Number One selection in this industry, the stock might be an excellent gainer in 1976–77 as takeover bait. Now at 16, AR may not double, but could come close to it. Some analysts prefer AR to Anaconda which was recently acquired at $27 a share.

Callahan Mining Corporation owns the Galena mine in Idaho, the country's second most productive silver mine, and received 50 percent of the profits from this operation. The company also has two manufacturing units, the Flexaust Company Division (hose and ducts) and Pathway Bellows, Inc., maker of metallic expansion joints. Callahan also is engaged in a variety of base metal projects and working interests in more than 1.2 million acres in the Canadian Arctic Islands, with participation in the major share of gas thus far discovered in that area.

CMN common is listed on NYSE with 3,545,000 common shares outstanding. Per-share net for 1975 was 80¢, down from $1.21 in 1974. Working capital at the year's end was $13,879,000. The stock quoted at 14 has sold as high as 35⅛. It could retrace that gain if silver moved up to $5.50 an ounce. Output in 1975 was 3,350,000 ounces.

Callahan also has a 5 percent interest in a large new Idaho property, Coeur d'Alene Mining Corporation, managed by ASARCO (which owns a 50 percent interest). A 450-ton-a-day mill is rated to produce 2.2 million ounces of silver, after startup in 1976. Coeur d'Alene has 4,181,-578 shares outstanding, trading OTC at 4⅞. This is a potential doubler.

Lacana Mining Corporation, formed in 1975 as a merger of three established companies, has 5,335,310 common shares outstanding. It is traded on the Toronto Stock Exchange, under the symbol LCA, and in the OTC market in the United States. The company, with headquarters in Toronto, is potentially one of the largest silver producers in North America. Lacana has four significant mines located in the Guanajuato district in Mexico, 240 miles north of Mexico City. The largest mine, Las Torres–Cedros, draws its ore from the same region where the Spaniards first mined silver 400 years ago. In the intervening years, over three billion ounces have been produced here.

The new mill at Torres, with capacity of 2,000 tons per day, serves Torres and the three other mines in the region. Lacana's share of this project is 30 percent. Two strong partners, Fresnillo, S.A., and Industrias Penoles, S.A. own 37 and 33 percent, respectively. Lacana also has another producing silver-lead mine, Encantada, in Northern Mexico, whose mill is being enlarged from 500 tons a day.

Lacana common, selling at $3.40, could become an active performer with any significant upturn in the silver price. It has the attributes we look for in a stock that can double, including strong sponsorship. DuPont of Canada owns 22 percent of Lacana common. Lacana also has extensive uranium acreage.

We are giving below some useful guidelines drawn up by Paul Penna, a respected mining executive in charge of a number of expanding Canadian mining operations, including Agnico-Eagle Mines Ltd., a producer of both gold and silver.

GUIDELINES FOR MINING STOCKS

There are four things to look for in any successful mining venture: (1) location and definition of an accessible ore body sufficiently extensive and high grade to justify and support profitable mining for many years; (2) a competent management, skillful in exploration, development and mine operation; (3) availability of dependable and reasonably priced mine labor; (4) adequate original capital plus the ability to raise additional funds, if required, for expanded operations or mill construction. Even with these requirements met you will need some luck to come up with big winners.

The ore body is, of course, the essential ingredient. A good ore body may be located (a) by surface prospecting of a likely terrain, (b) air-borne geophysical surveys, (c) follow-up diamond drilling to define the grade and extent of mineralized formations both vertically and horizontally.

For my money, Paul Penna's opinions are worth their weight in gold. It is important to bear in mind, also, that the cheapest way to extract ore is by open pit mining, but most mines use shafts (vertical) or adits (entering the mineralized area laterally). Whereas, forty or fifty years ago, mining might be done by individuals with picks, shovels, and a donkey, today mining is big business. The little mines such as were operated earlier in Colorado, Nevada, and Idaho are no longer economical. You must have a large ore body, modern machinery, and substantial working capital to mine successfully today, although quite a few marginal older mines are being restored to production, motivated by higher prices since 1971 for gold and silver. Earth Resources has an important American silver property, and Dankoe Mines is expanding production in British Columbia.

The investor should favor mines not too remote from civilization, with lower operating costs and shorter transportation of product to market. Some gold mines in Alaska and Yellowknife are not only remote but so far north that they can only be worked for a few months each year.

In general, ore bodies to be profitable should run at least .20 ounces to the ton in gold, and 10 ounces per ton or higher in silver. More important than these minimums, however, are the probable size and extent of the ore bodies. Long-life mines are obviously to be preferred by speculators.

COPPER MINING SHARES

We have devoted considerable space to mining shares because we are convinced that unusual opportunities for dramatic gain exist in this market sector in the period immediately ahead. Gold and silver prices slacked off considerably in 1974–75 from their record highs of $197.50 and $6.70, to $115 and $4.38 (September, 1976). These price adjustments have brought precious metal shares into a buying range and set the stage for confident upturns because: (1) rising prices are essential to catch up with increased production costs; and (2) there is evidence that worldwide inflation is in a lull but may resume anytime. Predictably, continuous currency devaluations in many nations appear certain to stimulate another upsurge in hedge buying, as in 1973. (Only this time, prices seem destined to exceed past highs. We expect gold at $150 and silver at $9 or $10 an ounce in 1977.)

There is also a new awareness around the world that not only gold and silver but the industrial metals as well, particularly copper, are sound inflation hedges. Prudent investors believe that, in the prevailing economic climate, it is better to own copper in the ground in stock certificates, than dwindling paper money in one's wallet or bank account. Not only do inflationary expectations point to the desirability of owning base metals, but major price advances from the depressed quotations of 1974–75 seem probable in view of the industrial recovery now in progress. If copper had no future attraction, why would Crane Company, Atlantic Richfield, and Tenneco have been so eager to acquire Anaconda shares, bidding them up from a 1975 low of 13½ to $27? (In early April, 1976, Atlantic Richfield announced that it had accepted six million shares of "A" tendered at $27.)

Yo-yo prices. In 1973–74 world prices for copper more than tripled—from a low of 48½¢ a pound to $1.52; and in 1974 the major companies prospered like Arabs. On a per-share basis, Anaconda earned $4.83, Kennecott $5.08, Phelps Dodge $3.15. In sharp contrast, the 1975 figures were dismal—minus $1.80 for Anaconda, only 66¢ for Kennecott, and $1.03 for Phelps Dodge.

Copper prices have turned around from their 1975 low of 57¢. On March 21, 1976, ASARCO, Inc. announced a 3¢

price advance to 66¢. This boost seemed not only appropriate but quite urgent because the average cost of production of a pound of copper in the United States and Canada is approximately 70¢. Marginal companies need copper at a minimum of $1 to make respectable returns on their investments. The most efficient producers are Phelps Dodge and the new Cyprus mine in Arizona which can deliver copper at approximatley 55¢ a pound.

Further, a sustained rise in copper seems justified by an improving economy. Copper is the oldest and one of the most essential industrial metals, used extensively in home construction, the electrical appliance industry, automotive, transportation, telephone, electric utility, and electronic industries. (Construction, which had been lagging, was up 16 percent in the first quarter of 1976.)

World primary and secondary copper consumption is expected to increase in 1976 by over 25 percent to 7.7 million tons, and to move up to 9 million tons in 1977. Total worldwide refined copper production for 1976 has been projected at 8.1 million tons.

Interruptions in production seem to be a built-in phenomenon of the copper industry, whether occasioned by strikes, by revolutions in Chile or Peru, or with respect to South African companies by political, transportation or border problems in Zaire and Zambia. Shutdowns of high-cost mines occur whenever copper prices plummet. In January, 1976, Copper Range (located in the Upper Peninsula of Michigan, with a huge ore body but with operating costs 20 percent higher than most other major United States producers) practically closed down, laying off some 1,600 workers.

Copper is by no means a scarce metal. If all the known sources (there are huge, untapped reserves in Chile, Peru, and South Africa) came on stream at once, copper could easily become a glut on the market. Not only that, but some mines, because of the richness of their ores and the low cost of abundant native labor, can consistently undersell the world. For example, Palabora Mines in South Africa can produce copper at 45¢ a pound.

In an imperfect world, however, it seems likely that the traditional impediments to maximized production will persist and recur, and that copper may be ready for another one of its major cyclical upswings. If so, the metal must now afford some good stock market opportunities.

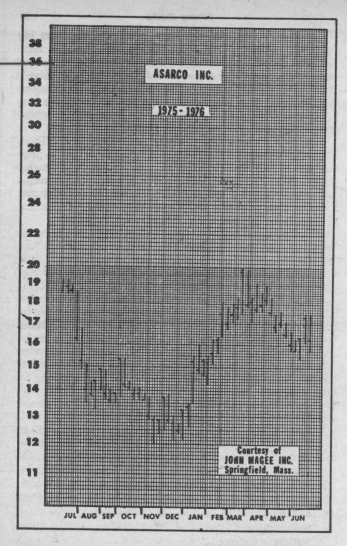

This chart represents the weekly range of stock prices, showing the high, low, and closing, of ASARCO Inc. (NYSE) for the period June, 1975, through July, 1976. Similar charts for other corporations appear throughout the book and show figures for the same period on the same basis.

ASARCO, INC. Of the large producers, the next big target company for accumulation and possible take-over might be ASARCO, Inc. It has huge smelting capacity (some of it outmoded, however). It is also a major producer, and the world's largest smelter of silver. In addition to American mining production, it has rich and extensive copper reserves in Peru and Australia. Further, AR (NYSE trading symbol for the stock) is in the lowest price range among the majors at 16. There are 26,801,000 shares outstanding. The 1975–76 price range was between 12 and 20. Aggressive buying of AR accompanied by ascending metal prices might give the stock a 100 percent price rise. In our shopping list, we regard this as an entry, but not a favorite. Between its high and low quotes, AR doubled in 1974.

FALCONBRIDGE COPPER LTD. In a lower price range, there's a Canadian company under excellent management and sponsorship that appears poised for lively forward motion as base metals gain in price. It is Falconbridge Copper, Ltd. While most American investors are familiar with such big copper producers as Anaconda, Phelps Dodge, Inspiration and perhaps Cyprus Mines, many have never heard about Falconbridge, a sister company to Falconbridge Mines and Falconbridge Nickel. The proper name alone has acquired considerable market magic in Canada.

Although copper is the major (and higher priced) metal surfaced, Falconbridge Copper, Ltd. is also a substantial producer of zinc. Its three operating divisions, Lake Dufault, Opemiska and Sturgeon Lake Joint Venture combined to produce 78,857,000 pounds of copper and 79,493,000 pounds of zinc in 1975. Total revenues for the year were $79,999,000 generating a per share net of a meek 5¢ on the 12,970,125 common shares outstanding. This 5¢ (earned on an average copper price of 55¢) compares with 72¢ a share earned in 1974; and $2.30 in 1973 when realized prices were much higher.

In 1976, however, the fortunes of the company improved. The rich ore bodies of Falconbridge, the improving quotations for both copper and zinc, and the efficiency of the mining and milling operations of the company all augur well for a resurgence of profitability in 1976–77.

In 1974–75 the diminished profit distillation led to a reduction of the dividend on the stock from 80¢ to 10¢; and the market declined, as a result, to a low of around 5⅜. At 7, FCL common (trading symbol on the Toronto and Montreal Stock Exchanges) offers interesting upside potentials. It is one of the lowest cost operators among significant North American copper producers, and the company has solid financial resources. At the end of 1975, working capital stood at $18,843,000, after expenditures of $2,536,000 on exploration and development and $5,224,000 in added investment in property, plant, and equipment. Unless Canada turns further to the Left politically, FCL has the ingredients for doubling its current market price by the end of 1977.

ATLAS CONSOLIDATED MINING AND DEVELOPMENT CORPORATION. This company is not only the leading copper producer of the Philippines but the largest in the Orient. It is a fine earner and a splendid dividend payer. Its shares are actively traded on AMEX under the symbol ACM. It is also listed on the Manila Stock Exchange and the Philadelphia-Baltimore-Washington Exchange.

The major business of ACM is the mining of copper ore and the production of copper concentrates. The native Philippine market for copper is far too small to absorb the 226 million pounds of copper Atlas surfaced in 1975. The company has been exporting for years, with Japan taking virtually all of its production until 1975. In that year copper prices fell and the recession forced Japanese smelters to scale down on their copper imports by approximately 20 million pounds. This reduction in Japanese deliveries in 1975, plus an expansion of ACM's output (by over 30 million pounds), caused the company to go after markets in other countries. It found them in India, Yugoslavia, Taiwan, Korea, and China.

The declining earnings in 1975 (to 44¢ a share from 62¢ in 1974) caused cash dividends to be suspended. Instead, the company paid three 25 percent stock dividends, and ordered another for March, 1976. Allowing

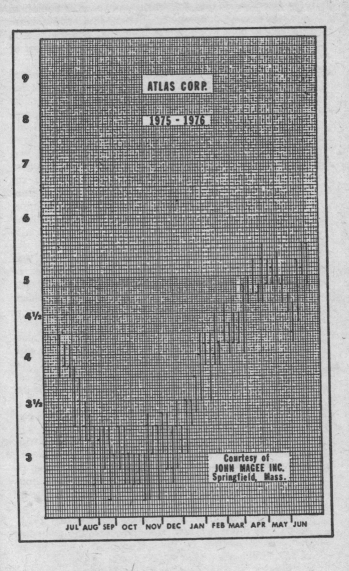

ATLAS CORP.

1975 - 1976

Courtesy of
JOHN MAGEE INC.
Springfield, Mass.

JUL AUG SEP OCT NOV DEC JAN FEB MAR APR MAY JUN

for these, ACM has a capitalization of $32 million in long-term debt, followed by 31,105,488 Class A shares (available only to Philippine nationals) and 19,061,000 Class B shares (10 pesos par value). Over 18 percent of the stock is owned by management.

Atlas boasts huge reserves—975,238,000 tons of copper ore, averaging 0.47 percent—enough to last for forty years at the current operating rate.

Looking ahead, Atlas has available another large property, Carmen. It had made plans to develop that ore body and to construct a related smelter-refinery at a total estimated cost of $310 million. This project was well under way in 1975, when it was suspended to conserve capital and to await better market prices for copper. The company also has a substantial nickel property, which it might develop, and an open-pit gold mine, scheduled to be restored to operation in 1976, with an indicated production of roughly 70,000 ounces of gold a year.

In several past years, ACM common stock has doubled in price. It might repeat the performance in 1977, given a new upsurge of inflation, along with the cyclical rise in copper that has been widely heralded. ACM Class B was quoted at 3¾ as this was written.

GIBRALTAR MINES, LTD. Another active copper property, this one in Canada, is Gibraltar Mines, Ltd., with 11,411,469 common shares listed and traded on the Toronto Stock Exchange. Gibraltar is a large-scale enterprise with a rich copper-molybdenum property in the Cariboo Mining Division, British Columbia. When it began production, in 1972, Gibraltar Mines, Ltd. had a debt of $64 million. This was all paid off by the end of 1973, and the company is now debt-free, with minimal capital requirements in the visible future.

Ore reserves at the four open pits, at the end of 1975, were 308 million tons grading 0.35 percent copper. This is enough to last 24 years at the current rate of production.

Gibraltar reported a $400,000 deficit for 1975. When conditions are favorable, however, the company can earn fabulously. In 1973, it realized a net income of $52.5 million, equal to $4.60 a share!

Gibraltar is controlled by Placer Development, Ltd.,

which owns 8.2 million shares of the common. Placer controlled properties have a history of paying out a higher percentage of cash flow in the form of dividends, so that this issue might become quite rewarding for income as well as for capital gain. From a price of 6⅝, it does not seem particularly bold to predict a quote of 15 sometime in 1977.

CONSOLIDATED RAMBLER MINES, LTD. A much smaller property than Gibraltar, but one with an unusually high-grade ore body, is Consolidated Rambler Mines, Ltd. Its producing copper property is in the Baie Verte area of Newfoundland. Reserves of the mine at the end of 1974 were 1,208,000 tons, averaging 2.51 percent copper, 0.07 ounces gold, and 0.60 ounces silver per ton. The company is favorably positioned to increase these reserves on completion of the sinking of its Boundary Shaft, sometime in 1976.

The efficient concentrator has a 1,000-ton-a-day capacity. Production at this facility has been edging up, averaging 591 tons a day in 1974 and 680 in the first half of 1975. Full-capacity operation should be attained in 1976.

Consolidated Rambler has 2,980,000 shares outstanding, trading at around $1.40. The company earned $1.15 a share in 1973. As a producer of gold and silver, as well as copper, Consolidated Rambler might generate sufficient market "moxie" to move up to $4 a share in 1977. Here's a mini-share long shot with a little meat on its bones.

Our stressing of copper shares is based on the historical volatility of these equities in past markets, and their sensitive historic response to improving business conditions and global rebounds in industrial demand. At the start of 1976, an aboveground store of some 1½ million pounds was slowly being consumed, and production and new mined supply were expected to be in equilibrium by the end of the year. Expectations of higher copper prices were also fueled by unrest in Africa, which supplies 20 percent of world copper. Match these conditions with some more inflation, and you set the stage for a bubbling market, and maybe a doubling market, in selected copper shares.

Chapter V

Growth Stocks as Winning Speculations

Growth stocks gained their greatest acclaim in the 1960's, when leaders of the clan—such as Xerox, Avon, IBM, Marriott, McDonald's, Disney, and Tropicana—far outperformed the more traditional dividend-paying equities and were clamored for, both by portfolio and individual investors at alpine P/E multiples ranging from 40 to 90. At that time the objective of many institutional investors was performance —maximum capital gains in a given year.

But later on, in the 1970 to 1973 period, glamorous growth stocks shed both their lofty multiples and most of their disenchanted followers. It became apparent that Avon door-to-door salesmanship could not expand forever, and that the Xerox Corporation, which in twenty years had run its annual sales from $40 million to over $4 billion, could not continue to expand at such a dramatic rate. The expiration of key patents in 1970, plus powerful new competition from IBM and Eastman Kodak, had begun to tarnish the Xerox image by 1976.

Despite this significant change in market climate, and in investors' attitudes toward growth stocks, there still exist excellent reasons for you to continue to seek out, and to select for possible speculative gain, modestly priced but authentic growth stocks.

The American economy was founded on dynamic growth— in population, production, new products, and in industries— launched by remarkable inventions and expanded by the drive of intelligent and industrious individuals to improve their standard of living. In America, the world's finest laboratory for economic growth, we have witnessed great structural changes and incredible gains in wealth and living comfort. Railways spread from coast to coast after the Civil War, and rail shares remained, for several decades, the favorite market speculations—the growth stocks of their era. Next emerged the petroleum and tobacco monopolies, broken up in the first decade of this century, followed by the huge expansion of the utilities in the 1920's. Then came motor cars and the revolution they created in peripheral demand for gasoline, steel, tires, electrical equipment, highways, and hotels—all setting the stage for an explosive and progressive migration to the suburbs. After that, the airplane spawned the jet set, making possible vacations in Hawaii, the Caribbean, or the Riviera, now reached within hours instead of days. Finally, TV, computers, copying machines, merchant chains, credit cards, and shopping centers have rounded out our instant and automated living style. Each of these advances spawned a new group of growth industries and propelled into prominence companies such as Coca-Cola, Singer, General Motors, McDonald's, CBS, Boeing, Zenith, and Howard Johnson.

The panoramic upsweep in population, production, profits, annual incomes, and stores of capital has now visibly flattened out, and we may not again see such astronomic corporate expansion as was displayed by these companies, or by others like Kentucky Fried Chicken, IBM, Polaroid, or Perkin-Elmer. There still remain, however, plenty of opportunities, even if on a less epic scale, for companies to spread their wings, to enhance their profits and net worth at unusual rates, and to contribute to our well-being in sophisticated innovations, such as heart pacemakers; companies have grown great and made fortunes for stockholders by the development and marketing of new wonder drugs, convenience foods, mass-produced housing, furniture, carpeting, clothing, entertainment and leisure products, not to mention solutions to such problems as the pollution of air and water and energy shortages.

The background for growth is basically the same. It hasn't ceased; it has slowed down and is emerging in different sectors, partly because our economy has now matured to a point (reached about 1970) where services account for a larger share of Gross National Product than does the production of goods.

Even with declines in the rates and areas of general growth, the characteristics of growth stocks and their attractiveness to investors in quest of capital gains persist. The most important attributes of any growth stock are a sustained and rapid rise in earning power; the reinvestment of most or all of profits earned; and an above-average return on stock-holders' equity. In other words, growth stocks tend to prove the market adage that "stock prices are the slaves of earning power." In the long run, they are!

A growth company should evidence:

1. Sales increasing at a rate of at least 15 percent annually.

2. Sales increasing faster than its competitors.

3. Net profits advancing by at least 15 percent annually.

4. A reputation for durability and quality of products and absence of hazards to their users.

5. Innovative ideas in products, packaging, or marketing (or in all three).

6. Capability in research and development, constantly improving existing and ideating new and broadly marketable products or services.

7. An assured reorder potential, as in razor blades, camera film, soft drinks, hamburgers, pen refills, prescription drugs, etcetera.

8. A motivated management and staff, rewarded by compensation, bonus, and retirement plans, and with substantial stock ownership by key officials.

9. Sound financial controls, moderate debt, and no recurrent liquidity crisis.

10. Absence of threatening foreign competition.

11. Low labor costs, and preferably a non-union shop (to assure no strikes, slowdowns, or walkouts that interfere with flow of goods to customers).

12. High earnings on net worth—15 percent or more annually.

13. Enough shares in public hands to facilitate an active trading market (at least 200,000 shares and 1,000 stockholders).

14. Market sponsorship—preferably by the firm that underwrote the stock, if it was a new issue: OTC market makers or an effective exchange specialist.

15. Plowback of earnings. This usually means no, or minimal, cash dividends, with declarations, if any, in stock. (This earnings retention reduces the need for outside financing or bank loans, avoiding interest charges that penalize profits.)

These fifteen benchmarks should serve as useful guidelines wh⟨⟩ you start screening growth stocks. An issue, to merit ⟨consid⟩eration, need not display all of these attributes; but ⟨th⟩e desirable equities and superior market perform-⟨ha⟩ve most of them.

Something should be said, too, about corporate size and age. In general a company should have been in business for from three to five years, and should have sales ranging above $2 million to qualify. Even though an issue looks like a growth stock, you have to be sure that the company has developed survival characteristics and does business in sufficient volume to assure and attract new customers and to finance plant expansion internally. The most rapid growth usually occurs between $5 million in sales and $25 million. If a company pushes its sales too fast, sometimes quality standards may not be properly maintained, and defective or returned merchandise will give a company a bad name.

Well selected growth stocks: (1) under proper market conditions should outperform more staid or traditional equities; (2) need not be traded in and out, because the classic gains are realized by long-term retentions; (3) should attract people of wealth who prefer, for tax reasons, long-term capital gains to cash dividends; (4) should evidence P/E multiples tending to rise at faster rates than net earnings; (5) should, during market declines, maintain their market values better than dividend-paying blue chips; and (6) should respond sensitively to reported increases in earnings.

A growth stock has an obligation, however, to continue its earnings uptrend, or followers of the issue will become rapidly disenchanted. Levitz is a good example. In the period 1968–71, it showed an annual growth rate of above 30 percent, but when its profit upswing flattened out in 1972, the stock tumbled 20 points within a few days.

By the spring of 1976, the annual rate of increase in earnings at Xerox had moderated. Certain analysts in Wall Street concluded that (1) Xerox had lost its leadership in the growth stock club, and (2) could no longer hold its historic dominance over the copy machine market, and was losing ground particularly to its most formidable competitor, IBM. XRX common soon reflected this viewpoint, and in the first four months of 1976 Xerox slipped from 68⅜ to 50⅜. In 1972 it had sold above $170.

Disenchantment is a relentless eroder of markets. Avon Products descended from a 1972 high of 140 to a 1974 low of 26¼. Polaroid, increasingly menaced by Eastman competition and in an earnings slowdown, melted in the marketplace. On December 31, 1972, the stock sold at 126⅛ (at an amazing P/E multiple of 90). On April 20, 1976, it closed at 33¼, at a multiple of only 17.

Likely candidates: service, technological, medical...

In addition to traders' disappointment over nonrising or descending profits, another force adversely affecting growth issues is the price adjustment in relation to net worth. Most growth stocks sell at a high premium over their book values. This corporate fat may rapidly melt away when earning power no longer can support or sustain an exalted P/E ratio.

There is no early herd instinct among growth issues. You usually have to search them out in the less traditional sectors of industry. They can appear in natural gas; in shares such as Houston Oil and Minerals; in convenience foods, such as Denny's, Pizza Hut and McDonald's; in Hartz Mountain Corporation; in Franklin Mint, Tampax, American Family, Colonial Penn, Olinkraft, MGIC, Carboline; Kar Products; Cross Pen; Millipore; Eckerd Drug; SOS Manufacturing; Burroughs; Moore and McCormack; or CBS.

Sparkling growth stocks are less likely to emerge in rail transportation, trucking, general merchandising, casualty insurance, publishing, utility, telephones, airlines, pipelines, beverages, tobacco, construction, cement or school supply industries. It is in the service, technological, medical, pharmaceutical, entertainment, mineral resource, or leisure-time sectors that we are more likely to find candidates for rapid market gain.

Another thing is that growth stocks often require from three to five years to flower and to fulfill their early promise. How does that fit in with "doubling in a year?" Most true growth stocks, when recognized in the marketplace, can rise briskly within mere months—and nobody says you have to sell a winning stock at the end of a year. It may be poised to continue its upsweep; if so, further retention may be indicated, or you can sell some and keep the rest.

In these comments we have endeavored to catalog the criteria for identification of growth stocks. It's now time to switch from the general to the specific—to select from the current market scene corporate shares that come closest to fitting the pattern we have described and that may speed as far ahead of the Dow-Jones Industrial Average as the fabled hare would have been ahead of the tortoise if he hadn't been slipped a mickey by Old Man Aesop.

Here are growth issues that we believe to be candidates for doubling:

AMERICAN FAMILY CORPORATION. American Family Corporation, headquartered in Columbus, Georgia, is the holding company for American Family Assurance Company, one of the fastest growing insurance companies anywhere. In the six-year period 1969–75, premium income of American Family rose from $12.1 million to $98.4 million. Premiums increased by 40 percent in 1975 alone. On a per-share basis, profits of American Family Corporation have risen from 51¢ in 1970 to $1.58 in 1975. This is quite a remarkable performance.

How has AFL (NYSE trading symbol for the common stock) been able to achieve such gains, and to outpace, in the rate of its new business production, the largest and most progressive A&H underwriters in America? The answer is concentration. Let's examine this feat in concentration.

Cancer care. AFLAC was founded in 1955. In 1958, it began writing a policy providing insurance protection against the heavy expenses incident to the treatment of cancer. At first, cancer care coverage was a sideline to the sale of life insurance, but by 1964 it became apparent that the cancer policy was the most profitable in the company's portfolio of policies. From then on, the dominant activity of AFLAC has been its cancer care program. Rapid expansion of premiums from this single source was achieved through development of "cluster selling."

Cluster Selling. This is a mass-marketing plan whereby the company's products are offered to individuals affiliated through trade and other associations, or through common employment. "Cluster selling" is distinct from group insurance in that sales are made, and policies issued, to the individual insured, although sales presentations are often made to many individuals simultaneously. Employers do not contribute to premium payments, and individuals may retain their coverage upon separation from employment or affiliation. The standard family rate policy calls for a $60 annual premium with a specific schedule of (fixed dollar) benefits defined in each policy. It is guaranteed renewable for the life of the policy holder. The company now carries over 42,500 groups, with premiums paid through payroll deduction or some other form of "cluster billing."

American Family is licensed to do business in 47 states, as well as in Japan and Hong Kong. The company has, at the present time, a virtual monopoly on cancer care insurance in Japan and sold 400,000 policies in that country last year. It has been estimated that 25 percent of the company's premium income may be generated in Japan in 1976. The company now has well over 2 million policy holders. (Also sold is term life insurance producing perhaps 5 percent of the total premium income.) The company has over 3,500 agents in the United States and some 500 general agencies in Japan.

Company agents are well motivated, and nearly 300 of them are believed to have earned over $20,000 in 1975. At the end of last year, officers, directors and employees together owned over 1,900,000 shares (25.5 percent) of the company's common stock.

Total revenues of American Family Corporation crossed the $100 million mark for the first time in 1975. Aggressive selling in 1976 is expected to expand gross revenues to $135 million or higher and to generate earnings per share of above $2. There are 8,107,098 common shares of AFL outstanding, listed on NYSE, and now selling at 11½, with an indicated 28¢ dividend. Quoted at about six times current earnings the shares might be regarded as attractively priced, considering the obvious growth characteristics of the issue.

Those viewing AFL as a vehicle for possible capital gain should also take note that legislation for a comprehensive national health insurance program might minimize the need for AFL's products; that a major breakthrough in the prevention or cure of cancer might make this type of insurance outmoded; and that other substantial life insurance companies might enter this field and seriously compete with AFL. These things do not seem to be early possibilities, but they should definitely be taken into consideration in evaluating this equity for the long term.

In the 1950's, life insurance shares were market favorites, sparking their advances by substantial increases in net income, year after year. AFL displays a growth curve to match that of the best insurance shares in the fifties. It is possible that AFL may distinguish itself marketwise, when more investors are informed about its unique merits.

GENERAL ENERGY CORPORATION. Since 1971, the company has reoriented its activities and sloughed off assets not related to coal, adding three coal mining properties: two in full operation and the third under development. In 1975, the company also entered into a limited partnership with Kirby Exploration Company for the exploration of oil and natural gas.

General Energy is currently producing coal from all of its three properties. The older ones, in Pike County, Kentucky, and Upshur County, West Virginia, accounted for nearly all of 1975 production. The Bell County Mine started production in mid-September, 1975, and is currently surfacing coal at a rate of some 30,000 tons a month. At full operation in 1977, the Bell County Mine is expected to deliver over a million tons a year of metallurgical coal—a commodity commanding higher prices and generating higher profit margins. (Steam coal now fetches about $23 a ton and metallurgical around $25, with higher prices anticipated later in 1977.) Estimated reserves are roughly 39 million steam/metallurgical tons in Pike County, Kentucky; 39.5 million steam in Upshur, West Virginia; and above 200 million of metallurgical coal in Bell County, Kentucky. Total production in 1975 amounted to approximately 1.2 million tons.

Prices of coal, somewhat depressed in 1975, were expected to improve in 1976 and in 1977, resulting from expanded demand for metallurgical coal in the steel industry. More efficient operations are expected to reduce costs in 1976 from about $19 a ton last year to $14 or $15. A production of 1.5 million tons at an average price of $30 per ton could translate into $2.50 per share or higher on the common stock of General Energy. For stability of earning power, the company seeks longer-term contracts (up to five years) with its major utility and steel company customers, with appropriate provisions for passing on cost increases to customers over the life of each contract. Management's goal appears to be for approximately 50 percent of sales under long-term contract and the balance sold at "spot" prices.

In petroleum, General Energy has an interesting limited partnership (25 percent) with Kirby Petroleum. Kirby, the operator, also has a 25 percent interest, and Bethlehem Steel, 50 percent. An exploration program on some 315,000 acres in several states in the Midwest and Southwest, is now under way, with about 35 wells drilled in 1975. General Energy, for its 25 percent interest, is committed to spend about $3 million a year for a three-year period in exploration costs. The payoff in this venture should start to materialize in 1976.

Capitalization of General Energy Corporation at June 30, 1975, was $1.4 million in long-term debt; 38,000 shares of 7½ percent Preferred Stock convertible into common at $8.25 per share and 24,887 shares of 6 percent Preferred convertible at $6.25 and 4,300,000 shares of common. At the end of 1974, stock options to management were in existence exercisable at prices ranging from 83 cents to $5.75 per share. The Murchison interests are believed to hold about 20 percent of the voting power.

Investors who believe that coal is the most promising of our fuel sources in the years immediately ahead might investigate General Energy Corporation. The common stock trades in the OTC market at around 11 and sold as high as 19 in 1975. The indicated dividend is 40 cents, supported by per share net of $1 in 1975, and expected to exceed $2 in 1976. Ahead lie prospects for significant income from the Kirby petroleum partnership.

If inflation resurges in 1977, then General Energy shares might be regarded as an interesting and possibly rewarding hedge. Beyond that, it offers favorable facets for sustained growth.

RUCKER PHARMACEUTICAL COMPANY, INC. This energetic producer of ethical pharmaceuticals must be well managed because its profit margin before taxes is around 35 percent. For several consecutive years prior to 1975, the company reported profit gains of 25 percent or more over the preceding year. In 1975, there was a sales shakeup and some leading company salesmen moved elsewhere, so growth slowed down.

Rucker belongs on a list of growth stocks because: (1) it features prescription drugs, and the company has earned a high reputation for product quality and reliability; (2) it offers a diversity of medical products including those for respiratory infections and cardiovascular treatments; (3) pricing and marketing are highly competitive; (4) products are sold, for the most part, with product liability insurance; (5) it is expanding its marketing in centralized urban areas in Southeastern and Southwestern states; (6) a newly researched product, P-200, a unique 200 milligram controlled dissolution papaverine hydrochloride tablet for cardiovascular treatment is believed to have a broad market potential.

Rucker common trades in the OTC market at 11, with 1,493,000 common shares outstanding. The company earned 79¢ in fiscal 1975 (year ends June 30th) with $1 indicated for 1976. RUCK (trading symbol) appears to have the potential to become a doubler, and possibly a glamour stock.

UNITED NUCLEAR CORPORATION. This company itself, and through its 70 percent interest in United Nuclear-Homestake Partners, is not only one of the largest United States mining producer of uranium, but an important maker of nuclear fuel ores as well. Its classification as a growth stock is based on the anticipated expansion of the generation of electricity by nuclear power. Another Arab oil embargo might make UNC (common stock symbol on NYSE) double in a hurry.

The company, which now grosses in the $100 million range, notably increased its per share net in fiscal 1975 (year ends March 31) from 8¢ per share in 1974/5 to $1.30. Rising prices for uranium and the possible major construction of new nuclear power plants around the world might rapidly enhance UNC earning power, which has historically been erratic.

UNC operates three underground uranium mines at Ambrosia Lake, New Mexico. Production (including UNC's 76 percent interest in the four mines in the same region of United Nuclear-Homestake) was over 115 million pounds of U_3O_8 in 1974–75. This will be increased by the new Church Rock mine and a new $27 million, 3,000-ton-a-day uranium processing mill now planned. Future ore supplies are being developed by a subsidiary, Teton Exploration Drilling Company, which holds mineral exploration rights covering approximately 34,000 acres in several Western states.

UNC also owns Plateau Mining Company, producing steam coal in Utah, with production scheduled to be doubled in 1976 to around 800,000 tons a year.

UNC common is preceded by $38.2 million in long-

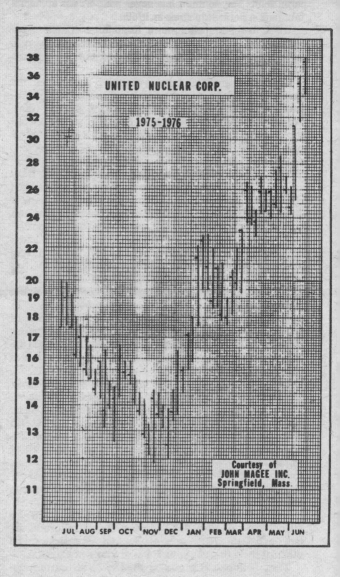

term debt. The common has never paid a cash dividend, but paid 4 percent in stock in 1969.

UNC has certain long-term fixed price uranium contracts which it hopes to revise profitably. Capital expenditures of over $25 million in the current year should expand the base of earning power.

UNC common has been a popular speculation for years. In 1976–77 it might break out on the upside, because our nation has done nothing to solve the fuel crisis. We are importing more oil each day than we did before the Arabs sandbagged us with a 400 percent hike in oil prices in 1973. Nuclear power may suddenly become urgent.

There are 5,933,590 common shares of UNC trading on NYSE. In the past decade, the price has ranged between 6 and 50. An upward move from 33 seems indicated on the basis of rising net earnings and a possible stock dividend.

J. L. CLARK MANUFACTURING COMPANY. This company does no direct business with consumers, but there are few homes in America in which its products do not enter. J. L. Clark has been a packaging specialist for 70 years, and today makes and markets a myriad of specially designed packages for over 800 customers. The foods of Kraft, Gillette blade dispensers, McCormick spices, Johnson & Johnson bandages and tapes, Maxwell House coffee and dozens of other household products come to you encased by Clark. The business is growing fabulously. In the five fiscal years (year ends November 30th) 1971–75, per-share net has risen from $1.83 to $4.41.

No one is more gifted or prolific in turning out metal and metal/plastic containers. The company has eleven plants in Pennsylvania, Maryland, Illinois, and California, including the latest at Bedford Park, Illinois, where spiral-wound paper containers are made for cosmetic, food, and fluid products. Current lines are being constantly improved, and alternate materials tested through a half million a year research program.

In addition to packaging, which accounts for about 80 percent of gross, the company makes industrial filters, and in Canada it produces drinking straws and other paper products through Stone Straw of Canada.

The company is strong financially, with current assets of $24.9 million against current liabilities of $7.5 million at the 1975 fiscal year end. Only long-term debt of $4 million stood on the balance sheet, ahead of the 1,281,847 common shares. This amount of shares was increased in May, 1976 by a 50 percent stock dividend with a 20¢ dividend indicated. The issue quoted at around 29, OTC, should continue to act as a growth stock.

NATIONAL PATENT DEVELOPMENT CORPORATION. National Patent Development common is a glamour stock. Founded in 1959, the company went public a year later. In the marketing euphoria of the late 1960's NPD (AMEX trading symbol for the common stock) sold as high as 67. Its appeal was based on the dozens of patents it was reviewing year by year, and the expectation that some of these might emerge into another Xerox, a Land Camera, or pacemaker.

More recently, a significant change has taken place in the corporate accent. Instead of testing and evaluating a large number of hopeful patents on a fee basis, the company now concentrates on fewer patents. It aims to develop, from them, products with broad market horizons that the company can either produce itself, produce with qualified partners, or license to substantial manufacturing companies with proven merchandising skills. Its "Hydron" polymers development is a prime example.

"Hydron" polymers. In 1965, this company arranged, with the Czechoslovak Academy of Sciences, licensing agreements to manufacture and sell HYDRON (Hydrocrilic) polymers and soft contact lenses throughout the Western World. These polymers, invented at the Czechoslovak institution, were developed as medical materials uniquely compatible with human blood and tissue. HYDRON polymers were also found useful (1) for absorbing water vapor on glass surfaces, and (2) for transport and slow release at preset schedules of drugs, chemicals, dyes and fragrances.

In 1966, the company entered into an exclusive licensing agreement with Bausch & Lomb, to manufacture, use and sell soft contact lenses in the Western Hemisphere (including the United States), Israel, and the Republic of South Africa. F.D.A. finally approved

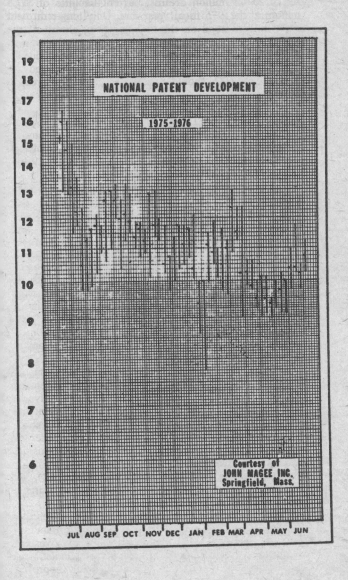

commercial sale of the lenses in 1971. The optical breakthrough and publicity about the new lenses stimulated a lively interest in the shares of both NPD and B & L. The arrangement with B & L was later disturbed by litigation, still in process, wherein National Patent has contended that B & L had attempted to monopolize the worldwide soft lens market, and otherwise breached its exclusive licensing agreement.

NPD is seeking antitrust damages in an estimated amount of $274 million. However this suit may be concluded, NPD itself is licensed to make and market soft lenses in many nations, and has a nonexclusive licensee in Japan. The company received $2,234,000 from B & L for the last six months of 1975.

Besides lenses, HYDRON polymers are used for ski glasses and eye shields of snowmobiles and motorcycles. The company's HYDRON Laboratories in New Brunswick, New Jersey are engaged in research and development on this novel family of hydrophilic polymers. The company also has research and development licensing agreements in this field with G. D. Searle & Company and other leading companies.

Other promising products. Other NPD researches on products with attractive potentials include:

(1) The GK-101 system—a chemical solution and a pump to remove dental decay, a device that reduces the need of dental drilling. (This was filed for approval with the Japanese Ministry of Health a few months ago.)

(2) Research on solid state electronics and solar energy, including development, with Massachusetts Institute of Technology, of systems designs for solar power. One application might lead to direct conversion of light into electrical energy, utilizing high multiple magnification of the sun's rays.

(3) On January 20, 1976, the company announced entry into the prefinal stage of its new Electronic Parenteral Infusion Control (EPIC) for controlling the rate of flow of intravenous solutions in clinics and hospitals. EPIC units involve a solid state control system and are believed to be lighter in weight, more reliable, and considerably less expensive than existing IV devices.

(4) The HYDRON polymer burn bandage, designed to reduce the incidence of infection in severe burn cases.

We could not begin to cover all the various researches being conducted by NPD or its new products in the offing. The company operates through eleven wholly-owned subsidiaries, the largest being Acme Cotton Products Company, Inc., which, at its large modern factory at Killingly, Connecticut, makes a broad line of health care products, including cotton balls, surgical dressings, baby products, adhesive strips, swabs, and a variety of first-aid kits.

Rising sales and profits. National Patent Development is a rapidly growing, aggressively managed organization; it excels at innovation and is steadily building up profitability. For the year ended December 31, 1975, revenues rose to $36,425,000, 46 percent above 1974, and net income was $1,738,000, equal to 20¢ a share on the 8,516,000 common shares outstanding.

Immediate targets are annual sales of $50 million, favorable conclusion of the B & L suit, expansion of the soft lens market, new applications of HYDRON, and rapid buildup in the sales volume of EPIC. If the company should hit upon a breakthrough in solar energy—that wouldn't hurt, either!

Regardless of the outcome of the B & L litigation, the company seems at a stage where it can expand and diversify its earning power significantly. Backed by a strong balance sheet position, technological and marketing capability, and an attractive array of sophisticated products, NPD has more reason to be classified as a glamour stock today than it did when it sold above 60 a few years ago. It is now selling at 8⅜, with 25,000 stockholders.

DANIEL INDUSTRIES, INC. Daniel Industries, Inc. (stock listed on AMEX, trading symbol DAN) has a product line in dynamic demand. The company increased its sales by approximately 50 percent in the fiscal year ending September 30, 1975. This expansion, matched with profits at an all-time high achieved in a recession year, justifies the company's membership in the growth stock club.

Daniel Industries, Inc. has three major lines: (1) mechanical and electronic flow measurement and control equipment; (2) alloy stud bolts and nuts (fasteners); and (3) water handling equipment, including pumps, tanks, and plastic pipe.

Measurement and control products are the most important. The company has been in this field since 1933, when Daniel developed and pioneered in the marketing of its Senior Orifice Fitting for natural gas measurement. This paved the way for an identification of the company with the petroleum industry, as well as to the design, production, and distribution of a sophisticated line of both liquid and natural gas measuring devices, together with electronic special purpose and read-out instruments.

Examples of Daniel's virtuosity in this field include (1) the metering and control equipment to service a one-million-barrel storage center built by Phillips Petroleum and partners in the Ekofisk Fields in the North Sea; (2) a multitube 20-inch orifice metering station to receive North Sea gas, by a 36-inch pipeline, in Emden, Germany; (3) a 420,000-barrel-per-hour metering and proving system for Arabian American Oil Company. Drilling activity in the North Sea, Arabia, and the Alyeska Pipeline give assurance of continued demand for Daniel flow products well into the future. In the North Sea, 23 new oil fields have been found in the past eighteen months.

Daniel Bolt Company is primarily engaged in making fasteners, specially produced nuts and bolts used by producing and processing companies in the oil and gas industry. Plant capacity has been doubled in 1975, and efficiency has been increased by a new heat treating furnace installation and an ultramodern fully automated production line.

The water handling and treatment products are developed, manufactured, and marketed by Ruth-Berry Company. Its business has been expanding, in particular due to the introduction last year of a new submersible pump line and to increased production and sales of PVC plastic pipes.

Other company facets include Daniel Services, Inc., Systems Engineering Division, concentrating on design, production, installation, and servicing of projects; and Daniel Industries, Ltd., which commissioned a new plant facility in Falkirk, Scotland.

Financial data. Daniel has documented an unusual

record with respect to increases in sales and profits. In fiscal 1970, sales totalled $18.6 million. In 1974, sales were $41.6 million; and in 1975 the figure was $60 million.

Per-share net has followed a similar uptrend: $1.05 in 1970; $3.03 in 1974; and $4.46 reported for fiscal 1975.

Corporate expansion has benefited from rising capital outlays—$1 million in 1970, and $4 million in 1975.

After a 2-for-1 split, there are 1,983,000 common shares outstanding, preceded by $3.5 million in debt. DAN common trades on AMEX at around 18, with an indicated 26¢ dividend (plus 15 percent in stock paid in 1975). The split broadened market sponsorship in DAN common and paved the way for its ultimate listing on the New York Stock Exchange.

Daniel Industries, Inc. is steadily enhancing its corporate stature and profitability, and is already recognized as a worldwide authority on flow measurement. DAN common exhibits all of the essential attributes of genuine growth stocks—in other words, the kind that can double in a year or less.

SAGA CORPORATION. Saga is a unique corporation in the restaurant field. It specializes in the provision of food services to schools, colleges, industrial firms, hospitals, and health care institutions, and has over 600 service contracts of this type nationwide. It is evident that Saga is able to offer superior meals at lower costs than these organizations can provide for themselves, and it relieves them of the responsibility of management. The company also owns four restaurant chains.

Expansion has slowed down in the last 24 months, and profit margins have tended to increase as a result. For 1975 (fiscal year ending June 30), Saga reported net revenues of $353.4 million, up from $294.8 million the year earlier. Earnings of $1.01 per share were down a bit in 1975, from $1.11, due primarily to expansion costs. In fiscal 1976, per-share net is expected to improve by 30 to 40 percent, as newer units stabilize their operations, unprofitable or marginal units are eliminated, and interest rates lowered.

Essentially, the Saga operational formula is attractive because in the food contract area the client supplies the dining hall and kitchen facilities and equipment, and Saga supplies labor, food preparation and service of meals on a management fee basis or a fixed daily price or rate.

The restaurant chains include Straw Hut Pizza Palaces (about 218 family style pizza restaurants, 154 of them owned), 30 Black Angus Steak Restaurants, 17 Velvet Turtle Restaurants, and 16 Refectory Restaurants located in Texas and six Western states.

SGA common is listed on NYSE and has outstanding 4,273,092 shares, preceded by $14.8 million in long-term debt. Assuming 1976 per share net of $1.40 or better, it might appear that SGA common is underpriced at 10¾ and could double in a consumer-slanted securities market. The stock once sold as high as 37. It is now at a stage to attract buying by institutions and is already held by twelve such organizations. Management owns about 40 percent of the common stock.

CAFETERIAS, INC. This is an unusual kind of restaurant company, operating a capably managed group of cafeterias, principally located in Texas shopping centers. Most operate under the name of "Luby's," but eight in the Dallas and Houston areas are called "Romana." In 1976, three new units were under construction, all scheduled to be in operation during the year.

The format is quite standardized. Units range in seating capacity from 250 to 320, are attractively designed and located, air conditioned, and fully carpeted. Almost all stay open seven days a week (for lunch and dinner only) and offer menu diversity and satisfying entree helpings. Most of the food served is prepared "in house," including bread and pastries, and quality standards are sedulously maintained by a roving quality control team.

Of the 40 units in operation at the end of 1975, 30 were in leased locations. Seven were owned by founders of the company and operated under contracts which deliver 45 percent of each cafeteria's earnings (before interest, depreciation, and income taxes) to the company.

The average annual total of sales-per-cafeteria in fiscal 1975 was over $1.2 million, and the combined units had about 2,675 full-time employees.

Growth characteristics. To document its status as a growth stock, CAFE (NASDAQ trading symbol for the common on the OTC market): (1) increased its total revenues from $14.1 million in fiscal 1970 (year ends August 31) to $38.25 million in fiscal 1975; (2) in the same period, net earnings per share rose from 31¢ to $1.32 in 1975; and (3) net income increased by 47 percent in fiscal 1975 alone.

Analysts who have observed the outstanding success of Morrison's, Pizza Hut, and Sambo's may note that Cafeterias, Inc. follows a quite similar pattern: attractive prices, quality foods, stress on operating efficiency, high profit margins, overall management competence, and regular additions of new and strategically located units.

Cafeterias, Inc. has $6 million in long-term debt, followed by 1,606,000 shares of common. The last public offering of the shares was 111,000 at 14 in 1973.

Assuming the historic rate of expansion of outlets and maintenance of high profit margins, Cafeterias, Inc. should continue to grow at an above average rate, propelling CAFE common from 18 currently to a higher price level in the months ahead. The present dividend of 32¢ might be increased. The stock could well double in a 12-month period.

S & S CORPORATION. The total response in America since the 1973–74 Arab oil-price ripoff has been unimpressive. Operation Independence, designed to make us, in due course, self-sufficient in fuels, did nothing but spawn another bureaucracy in Washington. Nuclear power? Communities, whether properly informed or not, worry about possible atomic fallouts, as a result, most plans for new nuclear generating plants are resting on the back shelf. Oil shale? Big noise, much ado about high costs, and no production of oil from shale in sight for years. Offshore Atlantic drilling? Still in the hands of the politicos. North Slope Oil? Two years behind schedule already, and no polar bears complaining about the oil slick as of late 1976.

So we get back to coal. We have enough coal in the United States to last for centuries. To step up production, however, we must solve environmental problems, dig deeper, open new mines, and provide more modern digging equipment. And we must build more railway cars for coal delivery. We're more likely to do these things than to accelerate petroleum output. So coal companies are moving forward energetically, and so is the company we selected for possible doubling, the S & S Corporation.

This company, headquartered in Cedar Bluff, Virginia, has been in business for 21 years. In the last two, however, it has been performing like a growth stock. The company specializes in the manufacturing and marketing of modern coal-mining equipment. Among its products in high demand are hydraulic coal trailers, the CX Coal Hauler, Du-a-Trac and Spartan feeder/crushers, the Mine Rover, a generation III Un-a-Trac, and a rock duster. Current models are constantly being refined and improved, and new products ideated, by a research and development program involving about $500,000 a year.

Coal mining companies had cut back their equipment buying rather sharply in 1974, so that S & S, in fiscal 1974 (ending June 30) reported sales of only $14.7 million and a per share net of 77¢. In fiscal 1975, however, the industry moved aggressively to step up production, and this naturally benefitted S & S. Revenues zoomed to $33.1 million, and per-share net climbed to $2.65. This growth pattern continues. For the six month period ended December 31, 1975, revenues were $26.3 million and net income per share $2.45 (almost as much as for the entire preceding fiscal year). For fiscal 1976, a net of close to $5 seems predictable.

The company has been improving and expanding its properties. The original plant at Richlands, Virginia, was substantially augmented five years ago. The Cedar Bluff operation was expanded 50 percent in 1973–74 and new units went on stream in 1974 at Marion, Illinois, and Washington, Pennsylvania. A new warehouse was completed at Pikesville, Kentucky, last year, and two more supply depots will be placed in operation in the current fiscal year.

Company business volume is derived more than 50 percent from sales of its several tractor units and about 25 percent from replacement parts. In order to have these parts readily available for swift delivery, the regional warehouses and the depot facilities mentioned have been provided.

The upturn of the business at S & S Corporation does not appear as a cyclical phenomenon but rather as a reflection of powerful global demand for modernized coal handling equipment. These are not the cumbersome underslung underground tractors of bygone years but rather the more costly front-end bucket units, safer in operation and far more efficient in coal production. S & S in the past has concentrated on the domestic market. Now it is aiming at major overseas markets, especially in South Africa and Australia. This points to enhanced corporate stature in coming years.

The company is conservatively financed with $4.4 million in long-term debt, ahead of the 1,436,111 shares of common, trading on the OTC market around 21. The shares appear positioned to respond to the resurgence of the coal industry to indicated higher sales and profits in fiscal 1976 and beyond, and to consequently higher cash dividends. All in all, a good potential doubler. (Since this was written there was a 25 percent stock dividend paid.)

Chapter VI

Real Estate Investment Trusts (REITs)
Speculative Opportunities in This Distressed Industry

The modern REIT dates from the Real Estate Investment Trust Act, which became effective on January 1, 1961. Not much attention was paid to this new industry prior to 1969, and until then there was outstanding no more than $500 million in market value of REIT transferable certificates. In 1969, however, this sophisticated realty security caught on. New capital issues of REITs totaled over $1 billion in that year, and over $1.2 billion in 1970. Shares and debentures were offered by many of the most respected investment banking houses, then eagerly snapped up by investors.

What were the attractions? This type of investment trust is somewhat similar to a mutual fund. It was designed to enable a small investor to: (1) participate in large-scale realty projects; (2) presumably benefit from continuous professional supervision of a diversified real estate portfolio; (3) enjoy a generous income, whether from high-yielding debentures (many of them convertible) or through ownership of certificates of beneficial interest; and (4) though the latter, to enjoy a unique tax shelter.

A REIT is a trust, not a corporation; it must maintain more than 75 percent of its assets in real estate, mortgages, cash or equivalents; it must generate at least 75 percent of its income from real estate holdings (mainly from rents or mortgage interest); and to qualify for its special tax exemption, the trust must distribute at least 90 percent of all its income to its certificate holders each year. When this is done, the trust itself pays no tax on income thus distributed and thus avoids the dual taxation inherent in most corporate cash dividends. Such distributions are taxable to the individual, however, as ordinary income at his or her own tax bracket rate.

The REITs were acclaimed in 1970 by the banking and mortgage fraternity because: (1) they made available a new and flexible vehicle for financing large realty operations; (2) the certificates were expected to provide investors with generous dividend yields—8 to 10 percent—at a time when seasoned common stocks were yielding 4 percent or less; (3) the elimination of taxation on the trust income passed through more money for distribution to certificate holders; (4) the trusts, because they retained and "plowed back" so little of their income, would need to come to the securities markets regularly if they were to expand their holdings (this part the investment bankers loved!); and (5) realty investment heretofore limited in marketability now offered sizable and actively traded equity and debt securities, many of them listed on AMEX and NYSE.

It all looked wonderful. But what a turkey this REIT industry has become in five years! The promise of sustained high income to certificate holders faded in a distressing number of cases, leaving elderly people, who had bought the shares to assure them generous retirement income, sadly in the lurch. The anticipated dividends dwindled or died, market prices dove, and even the debentures ahead of the certificates declined dismally; some defaulted. Anxiety and uncertainty continue as the prevailing mood in the industry today.

There are over 170 sizable real estate trusts, and 146 of these have publicly traded securities. As of April 1, 1976, however, only 48 were operating at a profit and paying dividends! The others were at various levels of solvency, near-solvency, or burdened with large segments of their portfolios not producing income. Many managements have been kept busy trying to figure out how to keep bank creditors at bay, how to pay debenture interest, and how to stay out of the bankruptcy court. The second largest, Continental Mortgage Investors, in January, 1976, defaulted on $508 million in bank loans and $46 million in long-term debt, filing bankruptcy under Chapter XI of the Federal Act. (Only Penn Central and W. T. Grant were bigger bankruptcies.)

This disaster area is Grand Canyon-sized. The REIT industry had, in April, 1976, a total portfolio of approximately $20 billion. Amazingly, almost 50 percent of all that investment was producing no income for the trusts! Further in the aggregate, the REITs owed $11 billion to bank lenders. Of these loans, over 40 percent were accruing no interest, and $7.5 billion of them were in some stage of revision or renegotiation. Of major equities on the market, you'll notice in Table II that 21 REITs listed on NYSE were selling below $5. All had sold above $20 at one time. What a downspin!

Yes, this is a downbeat story, but stay with it. Where there are ashes there is sometimes a phoenix—and your fortunes could conceivably rise with it.

First, however, let's see how it all came about. Doesn't it seem remarkable that this great REIT industry, which started out with such elegant sponsorship and broad market acceptance, should land so swiftly in such a financial doghouse? How could so many financial professionals, real estate experts, and mortgage specialists who assembled and supervised REIT portfolios make so many mistakes—and such whoppers? What sort of expertise do realty executives display when 50 percent of the investments they analyze and select turn sour in less than five years? It seems incredible that such bad judgment could have been so epidemic.

Some of the reasons for this debacle are slowly emerging. In 1971, very few persons in banking, real estate, or business generally anticipated the major recession that would take place in 1974–75. Business appeared good then, and there was not readily apparent any serious slackening in housing and office building demand. The condominium was (as it turned out) at the peak of its popularity, whether designed for residence, retirement, or resort living. No one seemed to realize that these compartmentally owned structures were actually being vastly overbuilt from New Jersey to Key West. If you travel today on Florida's A-1-A Highway from Palm Beach south to Hallandale, you will see dozens of condominiums in various stages of construction—steel frame, half completed, fully built but not landscaped or tenanted. You will also observe occupied structures lacking enough apartment owners or tenants to meet the operating charges. It will surely take another two years just to assimilate this Florida inventory of high rise residential real estate, financed for the most part by REITs.

Equally, office buildings are no longer in tight supply in such cities as New York, St. Louis, Newark, Detroit, Atlanta, and others. In New York, the flattening out of economic growth had not been perceived, and the completion of the huge World Trade Center Towers by the Port Authority made so much space available that extensive vacancies surfaced in privately owned downtown office buildings, several of them not completed until 1973–74. Uptown New York was not much better off, and real estate people were jolted by foreclosure of buildings in early 1976.

Adding to the adverse effects of the increasing economic slowdown and substantial overbuilding, was a structural defect in the whole scheme of realty financing—overleveraging. Because real estate prices had been advancing coast-to-coast almost without interruption since the end of World War II, and costs of new (or replacement) construction advanced by 6 or 7 percent each year, it seemed safe to arrange for construction and long-term mortgage loans at very high percentages of appraised valuations. Shoestring operators had a field day. Many buildings were financed with $4 to $8 in debt for each equity dollar invested. That was all right when the buildings could be adequately tenanted, or when condominium buyers were standing in line. But if the property had been built on "spec," it was headed for trouble shortly as lending banks developed acute liquidity problems. Soon, the W. T. Grant bankruptcy also revealed the possible perils of store or shopping center leasing.

Something should also be said about greed. The banks in the early part of the 1970's had plenty of money to lend, interest rates were high and rewarding, and the taking on of even a marginal construction loan beckoned when the prime lending rate was 12 per cent and the bank could get 18 per cent for 18 months from a (then) acceptable, albeit marginal, builder.

The lure of profit also had an impact on investment banking firms. The profit in underwriting REIT certificates and debentures was excellent. The securities were easy to sell, and a continuing relationship with a substantial REIT was desirable as a source of future security business. In order to grow, these trusts were expected to return to the market for further public financing with some regularity. Also, friendly banks and insurance companies sought public offerings of these securities because they either sponsored trusts or had certain subordinated debenture or equity financing to arrange to supplement, or fund, their own construction loans on specific properties. And, of course, nobody thought that so many properties could "turn sour" so fast.

Two Kinds of Trusts

REIT operations are technically divided into two groups: real estate equity trusts and mortgage trusts. Equity trusts concentrate on the ownership of real property, which may or may not be subject to mortgages or other liens. They may also invest in raw land (customarily leased out to produce income) or in improved income-producing realty, such as residential, commercial, industrial, or motel properties. A basic tax shelter for the equity REIT is found in the relatively liberal allowance for depreciation. Most newly acquired buildings are depreciated on the 125 percent declining balance method, which concentrates most of the depreciation within the first ten years. At the end of that period, when the cream of the depreciation has been taken, the trust may sell the property with the difference between depreciated book value and the selling price reported as capital gain and the profit taxed at the rate designated by IRS. It is the cash flow and not "net after taxes" (as in a corporation) which provides the basis for cash dividends in an equity REIT. Representative equity trusts would include First Union Realty Trust, Hubbard Real Estate Investments, Saul Real Estate Investment Trust, and Massachusetts Mutual Mortgage & Realty Investments.

The mortgage trusts operate in a quite different manner specializing in the building of diversified portfolios of mortgages. These mortgages are of two kinds: long-term and construction loans. Historically, long-term mortgages have been acquired and held principally by savings banks, building and loan associations, insurance companies, and pension and endowment funds. The construction loans have generally been provided by commercial banks, savings and loan associations, and finance companies. While the more conservative REITs have stuck pretty much to the long-term mortgages, many of them invested heavily in the construction loans lured by high interest rates paid by eager builders. These might run from 15 to 18 percent, with possibly a "sweetener" on top of that. (It is the trusts that concentrated on construction loans that have been hardest hit.) Among the mortgage trusts, representative institutions would include BT Mortgage Investors, MONY Mortgage Investors, Chase Manhattan Mortgage & Realty Trust, Continental Mortgage Investors, Lomas

& Nettleton Mortgage Investors, and Connecticut General Mortgage and Realty.

A number of trusts are hybrids with substantial holdings of both realty equities and mortgages. Several of the major trusts are sponsored by large banks or insurance companies. Others are shepherded by real estate companies and mortgage bankers, with a cluster of the smaller REITs independently launched, financed and managed.

As you view the dreary results of these trusts as a whole, and evaluate individually the prospects for success, subsistence, survival, or bankruptcy, among the issues on the market four important criteria stand out: (1) the strength and stature of the sponsoring institution or group; (2) the quality and capability of the management; (3) the kinds of properties owned or mortgage loans held; and (4) the attitudes and intentions of the banks that, by the hundreds, are now the anguished creditors of REITs.

Probably the most common reason for the decline or the actual failure of so many trusts is that they were too highly leveraged in the first place—too much debt, too skimpy equity; and in many instances, there was an over-valuation of properties for mortgaging purposes. (Also, there were a lot of structures that had little or no economic justification and were almost doomed to become "glut" real estate the moment they left the drawing boards.)

To illustrate the massive debt structure characteristic of REITs, consider the case of Continental Mortgage Investors, now in Chapter XI. It owed over $500 million to a consortium of 103 banks, and had $46 million in publicly held debentures as well. All this was on top of 20,838,000 shares of beneficial interest publicly held.

Another trust that "made it" into Chapter XI, Continental Investment, owed $61 million to a group of 16 banks and $42 million to debenture holders, ahead of an issue of 12,-941,000 shares (which sold at one time at a market high of 24⅛!). Ah, what a fall was there!

We have recounted above, at sufficient length, the sorry saga of the REITs and the descent of some of them into financial limbo. The purpose of all this was not to write a financial tragedy but to suggest that, after all this grief, there must now be several opportunities in this market sector for outstanding recovery and gain. Certain analysts have indeed gone so far as to suggest that REITs today are in much the same condition as the receivership rails were in

1933. In support of this viewpoint, there are dozens of REIT issues now quoted at well below $5 a share and at least 40 bond issues selling below 40¢ on the dollar—several of them still paying regular interest! A brief look at the list may prove worth while.

Not on the bargain counter, but sturdy survivors of storm, are the trusts sponsored by big insurance companies. There are five of them: Connecticut General Mortgage & Realty, Equitable Life Mortgage & Realty, Massachusetts Mutual Mortgage & Realty, MONY Mortgage Investors, and Northwestern Mutual Life Mortgage. These have been quite conservative in their investment and lending policies, and both Mass Mutual and MONY have a policy of listing, as nonearning assets, loans delinquent for sixty days or longer. On this basis on March 1, 1976, MONY had 7.3 percent of its assets, and Mass Mutual 18 percent, on a nonaccruing basis.

The stocks of all five of these trusts sell at respectable prices on NYSE; all are paying dividends, although in lower amounts than in 1974, and their long-term debentures sell variously between 65 and 85. At present levels both the shares and the debentures appear suitable for comfortable retention. There is a general belief that the elite life insurance companies that sponsored these REIT operations enjoy such prestige and stature in the world of finance that they would not permit their namesakes to flounder discreditably.

Equally, the REITs affiliated with major metropolitan commercial banks are thought to have considerable shelter from deep adversity by both the pride and the supportive resources of their sponsoring institutions. Among trusts with big bank sponsorships are Chase Manhattan Mortgage & Realty Trust, Bank America Trust, Citizens & Southern Realty, Continental Illinois Realty, First Pennsylvania Mortgage & Trust, BT Mortgage Trust, Barnett Mortgage Trust, and others.

For speculative purchase, the bottom half of the trust list is the place to look for turnaround situations and possibly dramatic recovery from distress. In general, we suggest consideration of fairly sizable trusts that still have some equity left, have evidenced capable and responsible managements, and that have a group of lending banks that were cooperative enough to adjust and renegotiate loans in order to keep their borrowers in business. It should be borne in mind that banks are not eager to foreclose on properties that are headaches. They would rather reduce interest and defer maturities than to try either to manage or to liquidate properties of long-term promise under current depressed conditions.

In combing over this list, we must be willing to consider trusts that may not now be earning the full interest on bank loans or publicly owned debentures and which may remain quite dependent on friendly banks as they strive to buttress their solvency and for restored profitability in the years immediately ahead.

Of the units that stayed in the profit column and are still paying dividends, we are impressed with Florida Gulf Realty Trust. It's not big (only $35 million in assets) and it's located in Florida; but it has managed to select its properties well. Florida Realty shied away from condominiums, and in spring, 1976, owned eight office buildings (all in Tallahassee), and 13 shopping centers (all in Florida except one in Richmond, Virginia). Florida Gulf Realty has 975,000 shares outstanding trading OTC at 12. A dividend has been paid for the past eight quarters. Florida Gulf Realty may not quite double in a year, but it appears in line for higher quotations. It sold as low as 6¾.

More speculative and probably a better bet for possible doubling is Gulf Mortgage and Realty Investors. It had a shareholders' equity in December 1976 of $24 million, even though about 60 percent of the portfolio was not accruing income. It now has a revised $91 million loan agreement running to November, 1976, at a minimum interest rate of 4 percent accordioned up to 9 percent (with a plan to make up for interest, currently waived, at higher rates later on).

We think Gulf Mortgage & Realty will survive, as its "classified" investments are nurtured back to health; and we like the sponsorship by Gulf Life Holding Company, a substantial Jacksonville based insurance institution. The 7.70 percent bonds due 1980 yield well at 65, and the shares at 1¾ are highly leveraged and could move up with a little luck.

Hanover Square Realty deserves a look because of the nature of its portfolio and because it is sponsored by a mortgage firm which is a subsidiary of W. R. Grace & Company, a billion-dollar industrial complex. Their portfolio is heavily concentrated on single-family homes, supplemented by shopping centers and office buildings. About half of portfolio assets were nonearning or producing income at impaired rates in December, 1975. The stock of Hanover—946,000 shares outstanding—trades on AMEX and once sold at 23.

Now at 3¼, it might double, with patient and effective handling of eight or nine troublesome portfolio items.

B. F. Saul Company is a long established Baltimore mortgage banker. It was the shepherd for B. F. Saul Real Estate Investment Trust, which assembled an extensive portfolio of diversified investment properties—motels, office, and apartment buildings. Saul Real Estate Trust has a good management record, with only 17 percent of its portfolio with impaired income production in its latest report. Three series of debentures lie ahead of the 5,658,000 shares listed on NYSE, selling at 3⅛. An interesting way to speculate in this situation might be in package form: $1.000, 8 percent debentures due 1990 at 40 (OTC) and 100 shares of common all for about $800. The stock might double and you could sell it, leaving you with a $1,000 debenture that cost you next to nothing!

Not as well known to Eastern investors is United States Bancorp Trust, sponsored by a major bank holding company in Oregon. That section of the country seemed less damaged by the recession and United States Bancorp Trust, investing in both equity and mortgages, kept the non-earning sector of its portfolio down below 30 percent. It had a 1975 shareholders' equity of approximately $16 million. This is a less harassed trust than most. Its 3,434,000 shares are listed on NYSE and appear as a reasonably hopeful equity at 2⅛. Compared with the historic high of 20⅛, doubling from here seems to be a modest objective.

For the daring, we suggest a look at Barnett Winston Investment Trust, sponsored by an affiliate of Barnett Banks of Florida. This appears to have plenty of problems because of its heavy investment in condominium loans, with over 75 percent of the portfolio in the nonearning category at the end of 1975. The hope here is that lenders will swap their loans for real estate or that borrowers may benefit themselves and the trust by tendering debentures of the trust (the 8¼'s of 1990 sell around 42) under a plan to liquidate their loans. Buying of the debentures, thus inspired, would bid their price up. And rubbing the tendered debentures off the balance sheet would improve the common stock, now quoted at 1⅛. Here again, a package deal might prove attractive: $1,000 debenture at 40, and 500 shares of the trust for $600, including commissions. The stock gaining 100 percent or more would be a welcome investment, and the bond with its generous current yield would be going up along with the stock.

Another plausible long shot among the REITs is American Century Mortgage, a Jacksonville based trust, heavily involved in Florida residential real estate. The 2,607,000 shares, trading on NYSE at 1⅜, will require patience because, out of a $156 million mortgage portfolio as of 12/31/75, close to $100 million was not producing income. A number of bank loan adjustments are indicated here and some swaps. With a little luck, the debenture issues, quoted around 42, may continue their interest payments.

Investors in this picture must place reliance on the continued growth of Florida with a few hundred thousand newcomers moving there each year. It is also thought that the major backer of American Century Mortgage, American Heritage Life of Jacksonville, would not want the trust to go into a tailspin. Merrill Lynch, Pierce, Fenner & Smith is reported to hold a 20 percent interest in ACM's mortgage advisor. ACM common once sold at 29! We don't think it will go back up there; but it could double.

It is obvious that REITs are a submerged industry, and that even partial restoration of portfolio values is going to take time. Further, REIT managements, so heavily in the thrall of commercial banks, must be most correct, diplomatic, and cooperative with their creditors. In the cases of REITs with strong sponsorship, the banking groups will no doubt continue to accommodate. The Chase Manhattan Trust, even though it has a downtrodden portfolio, has been able to get not only the Chase but a sizable group of other banks in the lending group to reduce interest down to 2 percent.

Friendly banks may indeed be expected to consider swaps in settlement of loan indebtedness, lower interest rates (with amounts deferred paid back in later years); and even further loans to assure payment on publicly held debentures or even to buy some of them in at deep discounts. After all, if a REIT stays solvent it can continue to be an excellent customer for bank loans for years to come.

For less daring folk, the debentures with their high interest rates and possible market repurchase, tender offers or redemption beckon. For the bold, a cluster of shares acquired at $2 or $3 apiece, while risky, might prove highly rewarding.

Finally, be prepared to hold some of your fire and to re-enter some of these REITs after they've "taken a bath," by buying the new securities.

To illustrate, Continental Investment Corporation filed in Chapter XI bankruptcy in April, 1976, and offered a plan to restructure about $103 million of its debt by: (1) offering notes and preferred stock to bank creditors, and (2) offering $3.5 million in subordinated debentures, $22.5 million in preferred stock, and $16 million in convertible preferred stock.

If you wish to make a deeper study of REITs, get the full list of them from National Association of Real Estate Investment Trusts. We think we've skimmed the cream from this huge vat of sour milk, but you may be able to turn up a few likely candidates on your own.

Chapter VII

Warrants and Options

Of all the marketable securities invented by the fertile mind of "economic man," none is more dazzling than the warrant. It is a negotiable certificate issued by a corporation entitling the owner to purchase directly from that corporation a fractional share, a share, or number of shares of common stock at a specified price for a specified time.

Most commonly, warrants have a life of from three to five years. In some issues, the subscription prices are changed (increased) at intervals during their life: $5 for the first two years, and $7 thereafter, etcetera. (The subscription price may also be decreased, by appropriate corporate action, to adjust for any increase of outstanding common shares by split or stock dividend.) A few warrants have no expiration dates. These are called "perpetual." Tri-Continental, Atlas, and Alleghany warrants are examples of this type.

The warrant is indeed the will-o'-the-wisp of Wall Street. It has no claim on assets, no share in earnings or dividends, no book value, and no voting rights. (Sometimes there is a redemption price permitting the issue to be called in prior to its stated maturity.) The warrant is the most exciting and volatile of securities. It can soar and produce fantastic percentage gains, or dive and become a total loss. It handsomely illustrates an old adage of Wall Street: "The farther you're out on the dog's tail the wider the swing!"

The warrant is generally used in corporation finance under special conditions. It may be given as a sop, or inducement, to stockholders, and sometimes to creditors in a reorganization, to compensate distressed investors, if only in a meagre way, for the losses they have incurred in a prior bankruptcy proceeding and to offer them some hope, however remote, of at least a partial recovery sometime in the future. In such instances, a certain number of warrants are usually offered in exchange for each 100 shares of stock, or $100 face amount of debt securities, originally held in the bank-

...pt company. Senior creditors in a reorganization do not object to the issuance of warrants to junior creditors or stockholders, because this procedure gives away or distributes no part of the corporate assets or earning power. It merely gives the holder the opportunity, at a future date, to deliver new money (without any underwriting cost) to the corporate treasury through purchase of its common stock. Furthermore, the subject common stock, at the time the warrant is issued, usually has a market value far below the subscription price of the warrant.

A REORGANIZATION WARRANT

Alleghany Corporation warrants, mentioned earlier, were the product of a reorganization. This railway holding company had outstanding, in 1952, a $100 preferred stock with unpaid back dividends accumulated to the amount of $113 per share. To induce preferred stockholders to forego their claim to this $113 (which didn't have a Chinaman's chance of ever being paid anyway), an exchange offer was made to them. For each $100 in face amount of preferred stock there was offered a new $100, 5 percent debenture, plus twenty warrants, each giving the holder the privilege of buying one common share of Alleghany Corporation at $3.75 a share without time limit. As a result two million Alleghany warrants came into being. They sold immediately (in 1952) at about $.75 in the OTC market at a time when Alleghany common was trading at $3 a share.

The price relationship existing between Alleghany stock and the warrant then, and during the next four years, classically illustrates the three peculiar virtues of a warrant: (1) it can far outpace the common stock to which it is tied in percentage of market gains; (2) it has a market value at a time when its purchase privilege is actually worthless; and (3) it always sells at a price above the mathematical value of its conversion.

To illustrate, when Alleghany warrants sold at $.75, they were technically worthless because no one would put up money to buy common stock at $3.75 from the company, when he could buy all he wanted in the open market at $3. Speculators gladly bought the warrants, however, convinced that sometime in the future Alleghany common might sell substantially above $3.75. Well, it did! In 1955, Alleghany common reached $11. At that price the warrant was actually worth $7.25 ($11.00 minus $3.75) but it didn't sell at that price—its market quotation was $7.875, illustrating the "overspin" we've been talking about. In the period between 1952 and 1955, the warrant went up from $.75 to $7.875, a gain of 950 percent on dollars invested, while the common stock rose from $3 to $11, a gain of only 265 percent.

The purchase of warrants, in bull markets, can thus create far greater capital gains on each dollar employed than investment in the related common stock for the same period. A rewarding warrant will rise from three to ten times as fast as the common. The idea is to start buying the warrant when it is selling at one-third to one-tenth of the prevailing market price of the affinity common stock. General Tire $60 warrants sold at $7 in August, 1956, when the common sold at $50 (about seven times more). When General Tire common, some years later, rose to $275, the warrant sold at $215. Imagine, a gain of 2,900 percent!

TOP WARRANTS WITH NEW ISSUES

Back in 1950 there were only about ten American warrants (there were many more in Canada) actively traded. As needs for corporate capital grew after the Korean War, the practice of issuing warrants as "sweeteners" in the offering of senior securities steadily increased and in 1968–69, when bond interest rates were quite high, the idea of adding a warrant became most appealing because it made possible the issuance of bonds with lower coupons—6 to 6½ percent—instead of an 8 percent straight debenture with no trimming.

To illustrate, in 1969 Cities Service Company offered an issue of 6⅝ percent debentures, with warrants, due in 1999. The issue was unique because each bond carried five warrants, not to buy Cities Service common but to buy a share of Atlantic Richfield common at $110 until September 1, 1972. It is customary for the warrants to be detachable, after a short period of time, so that the bonds and the warrants may be traded separately. Bonds such as Cities Service 6⅝'s with warrants were prevalent in 1968–69. They broadened the warrant market and made possible a diversity of investment among actively traded issues.

Warrants have not only been frequently attached to new

bond issues, but they have also become increasingly fashionable in equity underwritings where securities are offered in units, such as two shares of common and one five-year warrant at a total price of, say, ten dollars for the unit. This kind of packaging has proved attractive to investors, and issuing companies favor the practice for a special reason. The warrant, when later "exercised," brings in new capital funds to the company without any additional underwriting costs.

Examples. In 1969, American Oil Shale Corporation was financed by public offering of units at $7.50 each, consisting of two shares of common and one warrant to buy a share of common for five years at $10.

On June 17, 1969, Midland Mortgage Investors Trust raised $20 million by offering 1.6 million "shares of beneficial interest" together with 400,000 warrants. This "package" was offered in units consisting of four shares of common and one warrant (to buy one share at $12.50 between September 30, 1969, and September 30, 1974) at a combined price of $50 a share.

On March 23, 1972, North American Investors offered 30,000 units (a unit was a $1,000, 5½ percent debenture, with warrants to purchase 24 shares of beneficial interest at $31⅛) priced at $1,000 per unit. On March 15, 1972, Diamond Coal Company offered 10,000 units at $10 each, each unit consisting of two shares of stock and one warrant to purchase another share. On April 13, 1972, LCA Corporation offered one million shares of common at $40.75; and one million warrants at $13.75 each to buy common at $46.75 per share, until April 29,1977.

On June 17, 1969, Computer Radix Corporation went public with the sale of 80,000 units at $9.50. Each unit consisted of two shares of common stock and one redeemable warrant to buy one share for a three-year period at $5. The unique thing about this warrant was its redemption feature. The warrant could be called in any time after twelve months at $.50 (unless previously exercised). In this way the company had a device to compel exercise of the warrant (if the price of common were sufficiently attractive) before the three-year period was ended. On August 20, 1969 Multiplex Corporation offered 150,000 shares of common and 150,000 warrants to buy common at $4 in units—one of each—at $3 per unit.

Warrants as merger bait. When the conglomerates were

market darlings in 1966–69, it was only natural for them to design attractive (tax-free) exchange offers to companies sought for acquisition. In that period the most common vehicle for luring the shareholders of target companies was the convertible preferred stock. This vehicle provides (1) a senior security; (2) a cash dividend usually larger than that being paid on the common stock of the selling-out company; and (3) the hope of a possible gain by a conversion privilege into the acquirer's common. An additional sweetener, when preferred stock was used, was frequently a warrant.

Probably the most remarkable use of warrants in company takeovers was the offering, in 1969, of 980,000 warrants to purchase Investors Funding Corporation Class A stock at $28 a share in exchange (one warrant for one share) for the entire capital stock of Congressional Life Insurance Company of New York. At the time this offering was made, Investors Funding Class A stock was selling on the AMEX at 43⅛, giving the warrant an apparent value of $15. This is believed to be the first acquisition offer consisting entirely of warrants. (The offer was later withdrawn and Investors Funding has since encountered serious problems.)

Virtues and pitfalls. Regardless of their origin, warrants are attracting thousands of new speculators each year. As the most highly leveraged of corporate securities, they can make possible extraordinary percentage gains on a relatively small investment under the right market conditions—and "with a little bit of luck." A $100 investment in RKO warrants at $.10 each in 1942 (1,000 warrants) would have been worth $13,000 in 1946! (You might not have been able to buy 1,000 warrants at that price, and you might not have held them for four years, but such a transaction was theoretically possible.)

The down side. Bear in mind that all but a very few warrants have a termination date, on which they expire: one, two, five, or possibly ten years away. So the first thing you must note in researching warrants for possible purchase is the expiration date. If it comes during the middle of a bear market, then the price of the warrant may fade dismally, and if the subject common stock sells below the "exercise" price on the last day in the life of the warrant, regardless of where it sold earlier, the warrant becomes worthless! Penn Dixie Corporation Warrants to buy the common expired on May 1, 1949. Three years earlier the common had sold at $30 and the warrants (to buy it at $15) at $18, but just before expiration date Penn Dixie common sold at $20 and the warrants traded at a meager $.50.

On rare occasions, warrant maturities have been extended by special action of company boards of directors.

Warrants are not a one-way street, and you must be prepared to accept jolting swings down as well as pleasant ascents. To guide you in this tricky field, we offer five suggestions: (1) seek warrants that sell for fractions of the common stock price; (2) watch the maturity date like a hawk; (3) make sure the issuing company can ultimately expand or restore its earning power, because you'll get nowhere with the warrant if company profits or prospects are heading down; (4) select an issue with enough warrants outstanding to assure an active trading market; and (5) when you have a satisfactory profit, sell the warrant and look around for another good one—don't exercise the warrant.

There are about 500 different issues of warrants available, a few listed on NYSE, many on AMEX, but the greatest number OTC. A hundred or so have quite active trading markets, but many smaller issues may trade infrequently, and you may encounter delays in getting accurate quotations or executing orders. In any event you have a wide selection and are quite certain to get a winner or two, if you search persistently among issues in progressive companies, and buy at early stages in a rising market. There are many sophisticated market ploys with warrants: hedging, selling the stock short as a defense, etc. We think these moves are for Wall Street professionals and may only confuse the average speculator. There's enough money to be made in the straight buying and selling of superior warrants.

The following list includes two perpetual warrants and a screened assortment of lower priced issues of promise. From this group we would expect doublers to emerge:

Warrants Traded On*	Company	Exercise Terms	Expiration Date	Warrant Price	Stock Price
			May 14, 1976		
A	Alleghany Corp.	1 sh @ $3.75	Perpetual	2⅜	10⅜
A	Atlas Corp.	1 sh @ $6.25	Perpetual	2⅜	5
A	Bangor Punta	1.038 sh @ $53	3/31/81	¾	6⅛
O	Far Western Fin	1.184 sh. @ $22.38	11/01/79	½	6⅜
S	Greyhound	1 sh @ $23.50	1/15/80	2¾	16
S	Gulf & Western	1.136 sh @ $24.21	1/31/78	6¼	24

O	Diamond Coal	1 sh @ $5	12/31/81	4	8⅜
A	Textron	1 sh @ $10	5/01/79	16	26
A	UV Industries	1 sh @ $66	1/15/79	5	
T	Husky Oil	1 sh @ $21	8/15/81	6⅝	21¾
S	Loews Corp.	1 sh @ $27.23	11/29/80	6¾	27⅞
S	Kane-Miller	1.25 sh @ $19.40	1/15/80	8⅜	19

*A for AMEX; S for NYSE; O for Over-the-Counter; T for Toronto.

This list was combed from the current market. There are always new issues coming out, however, so be on the lookout for longer-term warrants or energetic companies, selected by using the criteria we have outlined above. If you are very bold, research the warrants of some sick companies that might, with rare good fortune, come back to financial health. For example, there are a couple of dozen REIT warrants that sell for pennies and could gain dramatically in a period of sustained inflation.

On October 4, 1976, 816,666 warrants of American Broadcasting were offered @ $13.50. These permit the holder to buy one share of common at $24 through January 2, 1982. These warrants are well worth considering, along with the others in the above list.

The choicest warrant of all we didn't list because it is so high priced and hard to buy. It is the Tri-Continental perpetual warrant to buy three shares at $6.43 apiece. On May 14, 1976, the warrant was 45 bid, none offered, and the subject stock sold at $19.

OPTIONS

In 1973, a novel speculative vehicle came on the market scene, the option; we refer in particular to the call option traded on the Chicago Board Options Exchange, Inc. (CBOE). It is a first cousin of the warrant and the lineal descendant of the old-fashioned "call," which used to be offered by special Wall Street firms known as "put and call" brokers. The CBOE option has the advantage over earlier "calls" of being actively traded on an exchange and thus instantly marketable.

A CBOE option differs from other security types in that it: (1) is not issued as a certificate or bond of any corporation; (2) has no participation in the sale, liquidation, or distribution of corporate assets; (3) never pays a dividend or interest; (4) has no voting rights; (5) is not limited to any specific number of units outstanding, (6) expires within a fairly short period—generally nine months; and (7) limits possible loss to the price paid for the option.

In other words, the call option is not really a security at all but, more precisely, a short-term contract between a buyer and a seller of stock, authenticated by a special agency, The Options Clearing Corporation, which is obligated to see that the terms of that contract are fulfilled. The same type of contract has been developed and traded on three other exchanges since January, 1975.

Each CBOE call option gives its owner the right to buy 100 shares of a particular issue of stock in a company of stature actively trading on a national exchange, and at a specified price and during a limited period of time. The purchase price named is the "striking" price, and this figure may be the current quotation or 5 or 10 points above it. The stock covered is called the underlying security. The party that originates the option and sells it is the option writer; the party that pays money for it is the option buyer; and the price he pays is known as "the premium."

The call option is usually created by the outright owner of a given stock. Suppose Mr. Bull owns 100 shares of General Electric selling at $50 a share. Although these 100 shares of GE pay dividends of $160 a year, Mr. Bull would like to increase his income. So he sells, on January 2, 1976, a nine-months' call option terminating in October on his 100 shares at $50. (All options expire quarterly on the Saturday following the third Friday of the named month.) For this option, Mr. Bull receives from his broker, let us assume, a five-point premium—$500 less a $25 commission. The option buyer pays this $500 because he believes that, within the next nine months, GE will go up. If it goes to 60, then he may exercise his option by putting up the $5,000 purchase price, and then sell out at 60. His total outlay will be $5,500 and he sells out at $6,000, realizing a $500 profit. What is more likely, however, is that he will sell his option for, say, $1,000 (avoiding any need to put up the $5,000 purchase money) and glean a $500 profit on his original investment of $500—a 100 percent gain in a rather short period of time.

From this illustration you see how options work. They enable the buyer to leverage his money attractively—for $500 he is in line to make the same gain as the person who has

$5,000 invested in the same stock, and if the shares sell off to, say, 40, his loss is limited to $500, whereas the outright owner would be losing $1,000 in market value.

Further, anywhere along the way, the option buyer can sell out at the then prevailing price. He might, for instance, sell when the stock reaches 58, and his option would bring about $800, and a $300 profit.

Going back to the option maker, in the instance given, he would lose his stock at 55 to the man exercising the option, which might make him a little unhappy (because without the option he could have realized $60 a share). Conversely, however, suppose GE slipped back to 45—he would still own the stock and have $500 extra in cash; he would then be in a position to write another option and repeat the process.

If a party sells an option without owning the underlying stock, it is called a "naked" option, and he will be called on to lodge with his broker money or securities assuring that he will deliver the stock to the option holder if called upon to do so.

Also, the option may be used as a hedge when an individual wishes to sell a stock short, and to limit his loss to the price of the option if the issue moves up against him instead of down.

The critical points to consider if you would succeed in option trading are: (1) the price or premium you pay for the option; (2) the historic volatility of the stock; and (3) the termination date (generally the further away the better, although the more time remaining until expiration the higher the premium may be). Animate, glamour-type stocks, such as Polaroid or National Semiconductor, will command higher premiums than more stable performers, such as General Electric or General Foods.

Options are traded on Chicago Board Options Exchange, and also on the AMEX, Philadelphia Stock Exchange, and Pacific Stock Exchange. On an average day, trading in options may run at the equivalent of ten million shares a day. The number of issues now covered by options is over 150 and increasing slowly. Speculation in this area has become a significant source of commission business for exchange houses, and trading in these has tended to displace trading in low-priced stocks. Speculators who thrive on market action love these options. Large corporation managements have also welcomed the expansion of option trading because it definitely broadens market interest and daily volume in their common stocks.

We have devoted considerable space to a discussion of options because they obviously offer opportunities to double one's money within a year. We have only given, however, a capsuled account. If you really want to tread grapes in this vineyard, then get moving and read some of the brochures on options available at brokerage houses; read one of the dozen or so hardcover books that have been written, in depth, on the subject. And examine the prospectus of Chicago Options Clearing Corporation.

Having said all this about options, we would conclude by observing that they are hazardous speculations wherein you are as likely to get "rubbed out" as to make a great gain. If the market is of the roaring bull variety, you can make a lot of money in a hurry on a very small stake. For most, however, options should be avoided because: (1) they are a sophisticated contract and require knowledge, unusual market agility, and fortunate timing; (2) they are not based on analysis of intrinsic investment values, but are essentially gambles on the short run direction the market will take (which even portfolio professionals cannot predict with any accuracy); (3) they create a mound of paperwork if you trade actively, and may drive your tax accountant up the wall; (4) they are so low priced they attract a lot of inexperienced speculators (willing to "shoot the works" on a few hundred dollars) who really haven't the slightest notion of what they are doing; (5) they tend to develop "overtrading" which is often costly to individuals but rewarding in commission business to customers' brokers.

If you are genuinely attracted to options, then study up on them and get in touch with a competent broker who specializes in this field. Our own view is that, in the long run, you'll be better off, and rack up more gains, through purchase of some of the warrants listed earlier, than by engaging in frantic option trading, switching, and hedging among various maturities.

Regardless of the above observations, call options are apparently here to stay and may shortly be supplemented by "put" options, giving you the contract right to sell 100 shares of some issue at a fixed price, rather than to buy it. These are obviously vehicles designed to profit from declining stock prices.

Chapter VIII

Of Multiples and Markets

By now you are well aware that this is a far "bolder" stock market book than any other on the market. We have presented investment procedures involving entry into high-risk, lower-priced stocks and warrants and, in several instances, unlisted equities of smaller and relatively unknown companies in quest of rapid and rewarding market gains. It is anticipated, but by no means assured, that a modest percentage of the issues chosen and presented in thumbnail outline, will double in price before the end of 1977; that two or three may soar; and that the average of the entire list will substantially outperform the Dow-Jones Industrial Average within the same time period.

We have examined the stocks that have doubled in earlier years and have considered a wide range of market sectors: industrial, mining, service, REIT, technological, and growth securities. We have assembled useful criteria for preferential selection among both industries and individual companies.

There's some further ground, however, that we ought to cover, to facilitate your making sound comparative judgments, and to improve the timing of speculative moves. First, something should be said about price/earnings multiples, which exist, of course, only when there are earnings! This P/E multiple, or ratio, is a popular benchmark in security appraisal because it makes possible comparisons between individual issues, and between the various stages of stock market cycles. There's nothing complicated about a P/E ratio. It is calculated by taking the total of the earnings per share for the most recent four quarters and dividing this figure into the current price. If earnings are $4 and the stock is at $40, the P/E ratio is thus 10.

In the spring of 1976, even though the Dow-Jones Average had risen above the 1,000 mark across the board, stocks had not performed spectacularly or been driven to dizzy heights. At that time, 80 percent of all the stocks listed on

NYSE and AMEX were still selling below $25 a share! That left plenty of room for price advance expectations, and is of particular significance to readers of this book, because we have insisted, all along, that the prime opportunities for high percentage gains are found in this particular area (below $25).

Equally, in spring, 1976, P/E ratios had not zoomed out of sight. The standard comparison is always with the DJIA. On May 14, 1976, the average P/E ratio for the thirty Dow issues was only 13.1, no big gain over the 12.9 multiple prevailing on January 3, 1976, and well below the historic 1971 high of 17.3. One list of fifteen glamour stocks, tabulated at the top of the 1972 market, had an average P/E multiple of 47.4. Glamour stocks are always supposed to command ratios far higher than the "smokestack" shares that comprise the DJIA. This 47.4 figure, however, was excessive, and later market sessions proved it so, with the result that the average of those same fifteen stocks was depressed to below 15 in 1974. As we mentioned earlier, in Wall Street "nothing recedes like excess!" Polaroid sold at 114 times earnings in 1972—and at 17 in 1976; McDonald's at 81 times—and at 25 in 1976. Glamour clamor reached its extreme in 1968 when IBM common hit $701, a dizzy P/E ratio of 161! It now seems incredible that people did not race to unload at these absurd ratio altitudes. Perhaps the lesson has now been learned, because IBM in 1976 was trading sensibly at multiples between 17 and 19, and other highly fashionable issues at correspondingly modest altitudes.

Our own view is that only a stock in a substantial company, in an exciting industry, increasing its net earnings at a rate of 35 percent or better annually, really merits a multiple of 25 or higher. We'd much prefer to buy lower down on the scale. For example, as this was written, 9 percent of all stocks on NYSE and AMEX were selling at or below 5 times earnings. That's a sector to explore for gainers—among issues that have not yet approached the escalator.

The foregoing observations, however, provide little assistance in the screening of issues of early stage mining companies, tired companies operating in the red or skirting the edges of bankruptcy, or newer enterprises whose earning power is in the future. In such cases it might be useful to develop your own idea of a reasonable multiple at which you might expect the stock under review to sell, when and if it gets into the profit column.

The mood of recent markets shows no tendency to drive up speculative shares to absurd multiples, and among income-type equities, many excellent utility and bank stocks are readily available at 10 to 12 times earnings. This evident conservatism may produce fewer soaring stocks, but it should also reduce losses sustained by exuberant and overenthusiastic speculators, who have distinguished themselves in the past by pushing stocks to the top of bull markets.

P/E ratio analysis should provide a check against "buying too high." Also, earlier excessive P/E multiples should seldom be used as "target" selling points in closing out an issue you now hold.

You can keep current in your thinking about these ratios by looking at the New York *Times* or *Wall Street Journal* stock tables, which list the multiples of the equities trading each day on NYSE and AMEX alongside of their price quotations. You'll generally find a few companies whose shares are selling at seemingly absurd ratios, but usually only when profits are a few cents a share. Most will conform to current ratio patterns prevailing in different industries. Merck, for example, has historically sold at higher multiples than Upjohn or Pfizer; GM higher than Ford; IBM higher than Sperry; and National Steel higher than Bethlehem or United States Steel. Copper companies and coal mines customarily sell at low multiples because their assets are "wasting" —constantly being used up by current production.

Finally, P/E ratios are not constants but variables. They are influenced each day by market confidence, volume and activity, and by the rise or fall in corporate profitability. A stock can gain in price noticeably without any change in P/E ratio. In most cases, however, and particularly with growth companies, there is a strong tendency (in bull markets) for the P/E ratios in a dynamic company to rise at a faster rate than the earnings on which they are predicated.

SOME NOTES ON MARKETABILITY

Because everything you do in Wall Street depends on prices, some knowledge of markets and their operations is quite indispensable. Markets determine prices, but the market for each individual stock is a law unto itself. Most speculators prefer to trade in the broader more active issues listed on the major exchanges, on the theory that, if they wish to buy, there is a large group of sellers available; and if they wish to sell, there will always be active buyers around. Active exchange markets and high daily volume of transactions are assured by the very size of the companies whose shares are listed, and the numbers of their stockholders. The prime market example is AT&T, with 577,618,000 shares listed on NYSE and over three million stockholders. Active trading is assured among so many share owners variously wishing to increase their holdings or to sell some, not to mention the thousands of new investors each year who are attracted to AT&T. AT&T trades on NYSE, and also on the regional exchanges across the country.

The NYSE and AMEX, as well as the smaller secondary exchanges, are all auction markets wherein shares are sold competitively to the highest bidders at a given moment of trading. On NYSE and AMEX, each stock listed has one or more specialists on the floor of the exchange who is its designated broker in that issue. These specialists are responsible for maintaining an orderly market in each issue assigned to them; they are expected to make bids for shares if and when there are no other buyers; and to offer stock when there are no other sellers, at prices reasonably close to the last preceding sale. Over 3,000 issues trade each day on NYSE and AMEX. The reports of sales, prices and volumes published in the daily financial press give valuable information of traders. Where many millions of shares are outstanding, trading by larger market operators is facilitated because they may buy or sell in 1,000 share lots without causing jumps or dips in price.

The big exchanges, however, have no monopoly on stocks with gainful potentials. Generally, smaller issues in regional companies with, perhaps, only 1,000 or 2,000 stockholders will be traded in the OTC market. These may be substantially underpriced, partly because they are not well known, are trading only 100 or 200 shares a day, and with rather wide spreads between bid and asked prices. These more inactive markets are drawbacks you should consider, but they tend to disappear over time. Companies may grow rapidly in size and stature, they may split their stocks so that more shares become available and in a lower price range. As companies expand thus, they may become better known to the investment community. They may come to market with underwritings for new financing and get written up in columns and articles of the daily press or in journals such as

OTC - Negotiated

Forbes, Barron's, *Financial World, The Market Chronicle,* or similar publications.

Smaller and younger companies with only a few hundred share owners invariably start trading in this huge OTC trading arena, the largest and most democratic of all markets. Here you'll find quoted, however infrequently, the penny shares of small mining or oil companies, tired old companies, or mini new ones struggling for survival, as well as the seasoned shares of such significant enterprises as American Express, Anheuser Busch, Rank Organization, Connecticut General Life, Bank Americard or Chubb Corporation.

All new issues initiate their trading OTC, even though an exchange listing is made shortly after public offering. Most of the 14,000 banks in America have their shares traded OTC. So are some 1,600 life insurance issues. You should not ignore this market sector, because many outstanding values are lurking there waiting to be discovered before they gain enough in size, stature and trading activity to qualify listing on an exchange.

The OTC market operates in a quite different fashion from the exchanges. OTC has no central trading floor, no open or closing bells, no floor specialists. All transactions are negotiated between broker/dealers over the telephone or by teletype. Transactions may be between brokers in the same city or with traders in any number of cities across the country.

The availability of stock in an issue, or the desire to purchase it, is customarily evidenced by trading firms when they list their bid or offering prices in "the pink sheets," a tabulation published each day by National Quotation Bureau, and widely circulated among subscribing brokers. Investors seldom see these "pink sheets"; but they are a Bible for desk traders at broker/dealer firms and for traders in the OTC departments of stock exchange firms.

Until the arrival of electronic quotations, a broker who had clients' orders to buy, say, 100 shares of American Express, would look in the sheets and locate one or more firms making a market in the stock. A phone call might reveal that one firm had 100 shares for sale at 34 when the market was quoted 33½ bid, offered at 34. A negotiation might then take place with the selling broker reducing his price to 33¾ and the buyer upping his bid to the same figure. A sale would then take place at 33¾, and each firm would send out, on that day, "confirmations" to the customer whose shares were sold and to the customer who had made the purchase. Each confirmation would report the number of shares, the transaction price, the tax involved, and the commission charge made. (NOTE: Be sure to inquire the amount of commission for each transaction. These used to be fixed but now vary with the practice of each broker.) Many OTC transactions are also concluded in which a firm does not act as agent, buying or selling in the market for your account, but acts as a principal, buying or selling the securities for his own account. In such cases there is no commission charged, the transaction with the customer will be at a net price, and the confirmation will clearly state that the firm "acted as principal." (All new issues are publicly offered by underwriters as principals and at net prices.)

The OTC market is now subdivided with regard to the size and activity of issues traded. Some 2,200 larger and better-known companies trade their shares electronically on National Security Dealers Association Automatic Quotation, called NASDAQ. Under this system, a trader merely presses a button on a computer terminal on his desk; dealers who make a market in this issue locally, or across the country, are instantly revealed. Then a phone call to one of these dealers can implement the actual trade. This saves considerable time because, before entering any negotiation, the seeking broker has an accurate picture of the current market. Each NASDAQ quoted stock has its own trading symbol. For example, American Express trades as AEXP.

The more actively traded OTC issues are reported each day in the *Wall Street Journal* under Active Stocks; and another thousand or so are reported in adjoining columns under the heading "Additional OTC quotes," giving representative bid-asked ranges for less actively trading issues. Beyond these are several thousand other stocks that trade less frequently. These are either found in the "pink sheets" or in trading summaries that show the last indicated bid or asked prices, perhaps weeks or even months earlier.

There's another special OTC sector called The Third Market, wherein major firms trade with each other in large blocks, often 20,000 shares or more, of stocks also trading on exchanges. These wholesale transactions are usually made at prices very close to the last sale of the same issue on the exchange.

From the foregoing, you will observe the diminishing progression of marketability, all the way from leading NYSE issues down to a ten-share transaction in the stock of some local bank or closely held industrial company. For our purpose—trading for gain—active sizable markets are definitely to be preferred, so that orders may be executed swiftly and without inordinate price swings between sales. Particularly when the time comes to dispose of a security, you will want to find eager active buyers and not have the broker fielding your "sell" order ask you sarcastically, "To whom?"

It is useful to keep in view not only the daily prices of the securities in which you are interested but also the direction of, and the most actively traded issues in, the entire market. Observe whether the major current trend is up or down, and what industries enjoy popular favor. Note the stocks that evidence the animate market sponsorship. Stocks often perform most rewardingly when they are in vogue, in the height of market fashion. A favorite pastime of professional traders is to follow the action of, and to prefer, stocks that are trading in rising daily volume, and at progressively higher prices. This phenomenon is usually regarded as evidence that a stock is "being accumulated" and heading for higher ground.

One of the best ways to maintain panoramic vision of "the market" is to scan *Barron's Market Laboratory* each week. This compresses on a single page data from the preceding week on: (1) the hourly performance of the Dow-Jones Averages—industrial, transportation, and utilities; (2) volume of shares traded on NYSE and AMEX; and on Midwest, Pacific, Philadelphia, Boston and Detroit Exchanges; (3) the most active stocks on NYSE, AMEX and OTC; (4) Dow-Jones P/E ratios, (5) foreign stock indices; and a batch of other weekly stock and bond statistics. Read that "Laboratory" page and you'll be on your way to becoming a qualified market observer. And you may also acquire an acute sense of timing, the most valuable talent anyone can develop when he enters the market to make a modest, or immodest, killing.

Chapter IX

Unpredictable Erosion of Corporate Earning Power

The need to take into account a whole series of factors, inconsequential in bygone years, that now may seriously affect corporate profits, corporate progress, and the price of corporate shares: product defects, hazards to health, environmental rulings, and similar "modern" problems.

The business of investing or speculating in common stocks has become increasingly complicated with each passing year. Fifty years ago, companies could go about their business, making products and money, expanding their plants and paying dividends pretty much as they pleased. Corporate regulation, except for utilities, railroads, and insurance companies, was a random thing. Many security offering circulars before the 1930's provided information that was often incomplete, inaccurate, and sometimes containing outright misrepresentations. In addition, accounting procedures were far more tolerant than they are now.

People bought stocks because the subject companies appeared substantial, their products or services were well known, or they were technological innovators. Popular stocks were sponsored by prestigious brokerage or underwriting firms, or recommended for purchase by the enthusiastic sales pitches of customers' men. Buying was stimulated by a 10 or 20 percent margin arrangement.

The corporations, whether big, medium or little, indeed operated with meager government surveillance or intervention. Great frauds could lurk behind stocks enjoying widespread market popularity. Such classics as Kreuger & Toll, Insull Utility Investments, Tri-Utilities Corporation, Associated Gas & Electric, and McKesson & Robbins were among the will-o'-the-wisps of that era.

The security laws enacted in the 1930's, and the arrival on the scene of the S.E.C. as a Federal watchdog, have done much to provide "truth in securities" and to assure more complete disclosures of corporate information on which investors might make intelligent portfolio decisions. Markets are more honestly run today, and much has been done to reduce the "head start" advantage of insiders who used to get, and act on, board room news well ahead of the general public.

This expanded governmental authority and regulation tended to reduce the risk inherent in stock speculation by narrowing the areas of investor ignorance. But it hardly solved all of the problems! We still can spawn an Equity Funding, National Student Marketing, or a Sterling Homex in which tens of thousands of deluded share owners "take a bath." It is reassuring to know that there is a broad spectrum of new safety factors today, in addition to the legal niceties of security issuance and proper accounting and reporting, that make these examples rarer ones. But we must remember also that many of the provisions adopted in recent years for the protection of the public are a two-edged sword. However worthy they are—and nobody except a robber baron would want to turn back the clock—they have no slight effect on corporate profits, and corporate profits have no slight effect on stock market prices. It therefore behooves us to give some thought to what these profit-dampening factors are, and how they affect our investment strategy.

Consumer organizations or government agencies may claim products to be defective and insist that: (1) these be either improved or taken off the market; or (2) that customers who bought them get their money back. The defects complained of may have been due to an unnoticed slipup on the assembly line, in inspection procedures, or they may have been deliberate. In any event, the sales returns, the refunds, and the lower prestige of the company, when the matter becomes publicized, may seriously affect net profits and cause a significant and immediate decline in the prices of company securities.

Guarantee of products is increasingly in evidence, and regulatory agencies insist that there be less fine print in warranties, and that they be scrupulously honored.

Within the past three years, Ford, General Motors, Chrysler and American Motors have, in total, called back millions of cars for the replacement, or adjustment, of original parts or equipment believed possibly defective and dangerous. When such recalls are announced and implemented, the costs of inspection and repair can make a notable dent in current earnings and dim any prospects that the common stock of the companies affected will double within a year.

PROTECTION OF THE ENVIRONMENT

More serious than the return or repair of a part or unit are the suits for damages if a product causes illness, accident, or death. Dozens of cases of poisoning from contaminated food products have led to million-dollar lawsuits. Salad dressings, canned goods, rat hairs in baby foods or confections, and seafoods, have all made the headlines and dented corporate profitability and reputations. Companies long in business have been even forced to close down. The case of Bon Vivant, once a leading maker of vichyssoise and other soups, is a classic example.

Drug companies have had, on occasion, serious problems with their products. Thalidomide, sold extensively around the world, was found to contribute to deformities in newborn infants and was taken off the market. Elimination of this product line, lawsuits running into millions of dollars, and a decline in the share prices of the major producing company ensued.

Another costly debit to earnings may be the money a company is required to spend to eliminate an environmental pollution created by operations at a given plant. A cement mill in the Lehigh Valley district in Pennsylvania was closed down permanently because the cost of the equipment to correct offensive dust dissemination would make the plant unprofitable.

We are all familiar with the catalytic converters now required; installing them in pleasure cars cost the motor industry around $200 million, not to improve car performance but to reduce noxious exhaust emissions.

Coal companies have spawned a welter of environmental and community problems over and above the traditional hazards and perils to which coal miners have always been exposed, primarily the "black lung" disease they get from constant breathing in of coal dust. Coal companies engaging in strip mining have denuded and devastated broad expanses of countryside, destroying vegetation and laying the gutted land open to erosion and possibly dangerous floods or land-slides. A coal company's dam burst in West Virginia a couple of years ago, washing out hundreds of homes in the valley below. The company regarded the burst as "an act of God," but extensive lawsuits against the corporate landowner en-sued. Such damages and threats to the environment are less likely to occur today because of expanded regulation and new legislation. Strip coal mining must now be acceptable to the community and must not permanently disfigure the landscape. After the coal economically extractible has been removed, the terrain must be restored with trees and vegetation so that (1) the area will not remain an eyesore, and (2) active erosion will not adversely affect the surrounding area.

All of these protective measures cost money and bear upon the profitability of coal mines. But such measures, not required (or enforced) in bygone years, must now be taken, even though they slow down our national program aiming rapidly to expand the production of coal, recognized as our greatest energy resource. We do not stress this because we are opposed to social progress—we are not—but because we want to inform you of factors that most investors fail to take into account.

If you are considering a speculative purchase of coal shares, make sure the company has already completed its plans to be a good citizen and intends to provide all required safeguards in its mining operations—in other words, that it has in-cluded in its profit projections the costs of restoring land devoted to strip mining and comparable measures.

Lumber companies are in a similar category to coal. Early in this century, timber operators would enter a forest, cut down all the good trees, leaving little but scrags and stumps, and then move on. This ravaging of woodlands is no longer permitted. As a result, timber is more expensive, since costs of ultimate reforesting must be included in operating ex-penses, adding to the price and reducing the profitability of current timber harvesting.

Along with coal and lumber enterprises, chemical and pa-per companies have been chronic offenders against the en-vironment. A sulfur-laden liquid resulting from the manu-facture of paper has been frequently sluiced out into streams, killing fish, polluting the water, making it unfit for drink or bathing, and disrupting aquatic plant life. One such plant on Lake Champlain was closed down when the unwanted effluvium could not be reduced to tolerable levels or disposed of elsewhere. Paper and chemical plants on the upper Hudson River have been guilty of water pollution, and in one plant a chemical waste, vinyl chloride, so adversely affected the river that most fishing downstream was discontinued in the spring of 1975 by authority of public officials. We are all also familiar with the extensive smog control now required of utility generating stations and the restrictions of the sulphuric content of the coal they burn.

Quite as serious as pollution are the conditions affecting the health of employees who work in certain kinds of industrial plants. On March 1, 1976, Dr. Martin Corn, Assistant Secretary of Labor for occupational safety and health, in an address to the Manufacturing Chemists Association, referred to "shocking episodes" of serious illness among workers handling arsenic kepone, lead, and vinyl chloride. He further said that his agency is improving its ability to detect "the more subtle invisible hazards of the workplace," and that "for the next two years all our new hiring will be health compliance officers." He declared that "some form of toxic substances legislation is urgently needed."

ADVERTISING AND PROMOTION

A number of government regulatory agencies have been bringing companies to task for inaccuracy or misrepresentation in advertising and promotion. There have been criticisms of sleeping pills that are not as soporific as advertised, and cold tablets less effective than their ads in newspapers and magazines suggest. Years ago, Carter's Little Liver Pills underwent a change of name because it was not established that they were beneficial to that famous organ with which half the population of France preoccupies itself. The claims of certain mouthwashes are charged to have been exaggerated. This insistence on truth in advertising, and the adverse publicity about the products involved, can lead to removal of products from sale, or costly changes in manufacturing and marketing procedures. It is obvious that any company cited for possible misrepresentation or overstatement respecting its goods will not find its common stock especially popular with investors, at least for the time being. Few "doublers" will be found among corporate securities receiving such negative publicity.

Certain pharmaceutical companies have made headlines

when the Food and Drug Administration has raised questions about the efficacy of some drug in the treatment for which it was intended; adverse side effects which the formulation appears to have caused are another source of big trouble. The end result has, on occasion, been removal of the product from the market.

Oral contraceptives have recently been a cause of concern. Citations and removals have, in a number of instances, taken place after a drug had long been in commercial distribution.

Among foods, cyclamates used as sweeteners and Red Dye #2 as a food additive in a myriad of products came under a market ban because of possible adverse side effects. The point in mentioning all these is that when the F.D.A. swoops down on an item, with its attendant adverse publicity, it is bound to reduce the profitability of the company and thus the value of its stocks or at least to dampen investor enthusiasm for the company's shares. Even after weeks have gone by and the stock market has "compensated" for the "bad news," it may take a long time for the subject stock to resume any dynamic upward trend.

PAYOFFS

In 1975, the investment community was startled by a whole series of revelations: (1) that many renowned companies had made sizable and illegal political payoffs to politicians seeking election; and (2) that international corporations were getting a lot of their business abroad by largesse to favorably placed purchasing agents or politicians in foreign lands. Carnation Company disclosed that it had made overseas payments of $1,261,000 over an eight-year period; Merck disclosed $3.6 million in questionable payments to employees of foreign governments during 1968–1975; Lockheed claimed it paid close to $24 million to spur aircraft sales overseas. Boeing, Northrup and Grumman were in the same situation. Many of the biggest and most respected oil companies—Exxon, Mobil, Gulf—all apparently engaged in similar practices. So did Tenneco, United Brands, and Occidental Petroleum. Such broad gauged use of bribery in the solicitation of foreign business was quite a jolt to investors, but it didn't disturb the markets in individual stocks as much as might have been expected. If only one company had been cited, that stock might have taken a pounding, but with so many in the same boat the declines due to sales "bàksheesh" ranged from a fraction of a point to two points. In a short time, these moral gaffes seemed to be either forgotten or taken for granted.

Equally, on the domestic scene, corporate corruption, while reducing investor zeal for the affected issues, produced no plummeting in shares. During the Watergate exposure, seventeen sizable corporations confessed to making concealed contributions to help re-elect President Nixon. Among them were Northrup ($150,000), Ashland, Phillips and Gulf ($100,000 each), American Airlines ($55,000), Braniff ($40,000), and Minnesota Mining ($30,000). Here, again, the consequence was raised eyebrows rather than market jolts.

Although this book is designed to bring out those qualities in an industry or company likely to make it popular with investors and to propel stocks to higher levels, it seemed appropriate to devote a chapter to developments occuring quite regularly that can depress or dampen the clamor of speculators for specific issues. If we are to isolate stocks that could conceivably double in a year, we must, as far as possible, be sure to foresee and avoid stock issues where Federal regulations, environmental problems, product defects, conditions hazardous to workers or customers, or political hanky-panky may depress markets, disenchant speculators, and foment market declines.

What the market needs for a stock to double is a boatload of good news, a good position in a "fashionable" industry, a reputation as a dynamic company, and innovative products or services that allure and fascinate speculators. Not many companies can boast all of these assets at any given moment, but these are the benchmarks to look for.

Chapter X

New Issues, Mergers, and Takeovers

The increasing dominance of institutions in the equity markets, especially since 1970, has made it easy for the blue chip corporations, "the sacred cows," to market new issues of their stocks quite readily. Smaller, younger companies, however, even those grossing $50 million a year, have a much harder time raising equity capital because droves of individual investors, who historically have eagerly bought such shares, have now either become disinterested in, or disenchanted with, common stocks. Most trust departments of metropolitan banks do not buy common stocks in companies where the total market valuation of the issue is below $5 million; and they much prefer capitalizations totaling $30 million and up. The golden age of the new issue market—the 1960's —will be a tough act to follow.

To illustrate, in 1961, more than 500 new share issues were offered in the United States. Going.public was the fashionable thing to do, and dozens of small underwriting firms sprang up in major cities and became mini-investment bankers. While large seasoned companies came to Wall Street for large-scale stock financing, the newcomers in the 1960's were the market darlings. Avid speculators imagined each new low price issue to be an embryonic Xerox, Syntex, University Computer, Pfizer, or Zenith and scrambled to get on the client list of such firms as S. D. Fuller & Company, Peter Morgan & Company, Gianis & Company, etcetera. The 500 issues referred to above did not include some 329 Regulation A offerings in that year. "Reg A's," were new issues raising not more than $300,000 in new capital, and they were permitted to solicit buyers by means of a "short form" prospectus. This cost less to prepare and print and contained much less complete corporate information than the "full registration" prospectus required to be prepared and submitted to S.E.C. for review in offerings of over $300,000. The typical "Reg A" was an issue of 100,000 shares of common at $3. The "hot" companies were in computers, nursing homes, offshore oil drilling, pollution control, and space age and scientific research. Those with any glamour at all were immediately oversubscribed and went "out the window" as hundreds of speculators sent in substantial subscriptions for the relatively few shares available.

Stocks went up not because of any remarkable intrinsic value, or any exciting record of earnings, but merely because the offering was brand new; when it was advertised there were five buyers around for every 100 shares that were finally confirmed. Speculators and underwriters had a field day, and the new stock usually traded frantically for a couple of weeks. When the glamour of the offering wore off, however, people lost interest; two or three years later, the stock might languish for want of sponsorship, frequently because the underwriting firm had gone out of business.

By 1967, this seething new issue market had matured considerably. Of 162 full registration offerings in that year, the average size was 230,000 shares, and the average offering price approximately $12. A high percentage of all these new 1967 offerings sold to instant premiums, and several issues soared dramatically. Cordis, offered at $55, closed the year at 152; Optics Technology rose from $12 to $43½. Wang Laboratories from $12½ to $66. The lure of new companies, burgeoning sales expectations, and exciting technologies, coupled with small capitalizations and glowing publicity, were all that was needed to double or treble share quotations within a few months. Because most of these issues were larger, and in more established companies, they retained their market followings far better than the earlier spate of "Reg A's."

By 1968, however, the new issue market had peaked, and speculators lacking in market agility and unprepared for descending markets hung on while their "dreamboat" stocks melted in price. By 1974, confidence in stocks in all categories had waned, and new issues of the sort we've just mentioned became rarities.

The waning of investor interest in these new, romantic, and volatile issues, trading for the most part in the OTC market, has meant that many companies could not make public stock offerings and had to finance themselves by bank loans or debt securities. This created lopsided capitalizations and heavy interest charges, at the highest rates prevailing in a century. Very few companies went public in 1973, and many well-established corporations that had planned to do so withdrew their registrations. Managements were averse to dilute common stock equity by selling shares at historically low prices and at sizable discounts from book values.

The vigorous stock market which emerged early in 1976 set the stage for a visible revival in new equity issues which could then be offered at prices acceptable to both the company and to investors. Responsible for these offerings were the balance sheets of dozens of important companies top-heavy with bank loans and ripe for equity financing. New issues by J. P. Morgan & Company, Coors Brewing, a cluster of electric utility companies, and some newcomers such as Entenmann's Bakeries renewed interest in new issue among individual investors and brought forth many public offerings of companies of some stature. These offerings differed from the equity offerings of a decade earlier in that, often large issues did not represent new financing but represented rather the payoff of bank loans, frequently coupled with "secondary" offerings of shares for the account of selling stockholders. This latter type of offering tends to create the suspicion that if large "inside" stockholders were selling out they did not expect the stock to advance significantly beyond the offering price.

Typical 1976 offerings were National Mine Service Company, 900,000 shares at $16.75, to repay $7.5 million in short-term debt and to augment working capital; Information Magnetics Corporation, 620,521 common at $7.50 to repay debt and augment working capital for this maker of magnetic discs and tape recording heads; Public Service Company of Indiana, Inc., 1,700,000 shares of common at $26 to provide additional capital and bring equity/debt ratio into more satisfactory alignment; and Olinkraft, Inc., 1,000,000 shares of common at 32 to expand its papermaking capacity; and S. S. Kresge Company, 5,000,000 shares of common at 36½.

The question we wish to resolve here is the relative attractiveness of new issues. If a company comes to the market for the first time, then its shares may indeed present a unique buying opportunity, because the company, heretofore unheralded, may have a dynamic product line and a remarkable growth rate. When Franklin Mint, Wang Laboratories, and Loral Electronics "went public," they were in this high glamour category.

Then, too, you must consider the price of the new offering. Are you getting a good value or are you buying a stock that you should have bought months earlier—before it "got popular" or had expanded its sales and profits to such levels that investment bankers thought the company displayed adequate stature for a sizable offering?

Along these lines we have two case histories to offer. The first is Microdata Corporation, a progressive company in mini-computers. In my feature column in *The Market Chronicle* of October 16, 1975, this company was discussed, and its status as the world's leader in microprogrammable mini-computers cited; also its rapid expansion of sales from $6.4 million in fiscal 1972 to $15.7 million for fiscal 1975 was outlined. The stock was quoted at the time at $6 a share in the OTC market. The article concluded: "For those individuals . . . who prefer authentic growth stocks as vehicles for long-term capital gain, then a current consideration of the merits in Microdata common is suggested." That was in October, 1975.

Four months later, on February 27, 1976, there was a public offering of 500,000 shares of Microdata common at $19.625 per share! It was a "hot" issue and sold out quickly. Our query is, however, why weren't brokers and dealers telling about the merits of MICD (OTC trading symbol) at $6 and on the way up rather than waiting to sing its praises at 19⅝ after it had already gained 200 percent? It moved up to the low 20's after the public offering, but somebody else, not the Johnny-Come-Lately offering-day subscribers, made the big score in the stock.

Let's look at another example: Hy-Gain Electronics Corporation. Under a prospectus dated March 31, 1976, the company publicly offered 1,000,000 shares at $19.25, raising (gross) $21,179,000. Of that amount, the net proceeds from 500,000 shares went to the company to reduce bank debt, fund certain additions to plant and equipment, and increase working capital. The proceeds of the second 500,000 shares went to selling shareholders. Their "take" was $9 million!

Hy-Gain had attracted wide attention as a significant factor in the production of Citizen Band radios and a broad line of electronic communications products. Its sales had soared in five years from $5,738,481 (in 1971) to $34,605,174 in 1975, and in the same period earnings went from a loss of $53,448 to net earnings of $3,725,134 in fiscal 1975. Quite a record, and good "numbers" on which to predicate a popular public offering. The industry was hot, what with an indicated demand for CB radios of several million units.

This issue was not a first offering, however. The stock had been trading in the OTC market for some time. In 1974, it was never higher than 38¢ bid, and a year before the public offering it was selling at $2. We do not suggest that Hy-Gain is now a grossly overpriced stock, but we think investors should be just a little crestfallen that this issue was not directed to their attention at $2, $5, or even $10, rather than trundled out at 19¼.

From the foregoing, we derive these guidelines about new issues: (1) you probably should not wax ecstatic about one when officers and directors are selling out a bundle; (2) if it's not a new offering, look back and see where this issue has been selling; (3) it's better if the issue is to provide additional new capital rather than merely bail out bank loans and create a better balance between debt and equity; (4) prefer original new issues where the past record features innovative products or services and the present management people are major stockholders; (5) compare the price, the P/E ratio, and book value per share with another representative company in the same field; (6) prefer companies in business for five or more years and grossing over $2 million; (7) remember that brokerage firms and their salesmen make higher commissions selling new issues than taking your commission order for shares already trading on the market.

Each year, if you watch the papers and note advance registration of new issues with the S.E.C., you may find some excellent shares to which you should subscribe. Some have the potential to double in a reasonable period of time. Get the prospectus, learn all you can about the company, and you may have another Disney.

SPECIAL SITUATIONS: ACQUISITIONS, BUY-INS, AND STOCK SPLITS

A unique area of operation, for those seeking capital gains, is in corporate acquisitions. In the golden era of conglomerates, in the 1960's, the name of the game was the tax-free exchange. A large and aggressive company with adequate financial resources, a lot of nerve, a desire to enhance its stature at a dramatic rate, and with an actively traded common stock, would boldly single out a company it desired to acquire. Then it would propose an exchange of shares, with the acquiring company offering its shares for the shares of the target company, under terms (usually) whereby the selling shareholders improved the market values and often the dividend income of their holdings by their acceptance. Most of the time, the exchange was one common stock for another on a carefully worked out ratio; but occasionally a preferred, or a convertible preferred stock, might be offered to the target company holders. In this way, by making the exchange they would be getting the senior security of a larger company in place of common and receive a more reliable and higher dividend income from the preferred shares they acquired by exchange. Many of these offers seemed attractive at the time, and acquisitions by the dozens were consummated. Later on, however, if the grabby conglomerate failed to enhance or even to maintain profitability, its common and preferred shares faded in market price. In many instances, the person who had exchanged his stock wished he had never listened to "the pitch," and that he or she had hung on to the shares of the formerly independent company.

So much for the takeovers of a bygone period. Now, share for share exchanges are far less popular. The current technique is for acquisitive companies to make a cash offer—so many dollars a share—for the company they have decided to move in on.

In 1975–76, almost every week, such cash offers were announced in the financial pages, often coming in "out of the blue" with no advance notice to the target company or its management that anyone was even looking for its stock. What prompts these bold bids? How does one company decide that another one is so instantly desirable?

There are many plausible reasons. The aggressor company may state or allege: (1) that it wishes to rescue the shareholders of the sought company from an incompetent management; (2) that it is in a position notably to increase the earning power of the subject company by a merger; (3) that it desires the particular management capability, product line, manufacturing facilities, or market coverage of the sought company; (4) that the price it offers is substantially above the recent trading range of the seller's shares; (5) that the offer assures the seller of a premium over book value; (6) that consolidated operation of the properties could expand total profitability; (7) that the cash offer may enable the recipient to bail out of a stock he has held at a loss for years or give him a desirable capital gain.

However plausible and even winning these arguments may be, corporate "raiding" of this sort seems to be unpopular in many quarters. It is argued that in many instances old and faithful employees of the selling company are "dumped." Further, the imposition of a new "outside" management team discourages faithful old employees from exerting themselves, inhibits their best efforts, and stifles their desire to present new ideas or to achieve higher efficiency. Rather, while the offer is being made, the time of personnel, all the way down from the executive suite, may be spent trying to combat the "raider's" offer and to make sure that it does not succeed. Often the defensive steps will include extensive publicity efforts to discredit the offer and the company making it or legal action to impede, delay or block it.

Business consultants, securities analysts, and economists may also argue that the proposed acquisition will achieve no long-term benefits and that all or most of the advantages claimed by the buying company might be achieved—short of merger—merely by working agreements and intercompany production or sales contracts. Further, these observers contend that it is unfair to stockholders of the sought company to be asked to accept on short notice a fixed price for their holdings when (1) the price offered is not truly adequate, or (2) greater long-run benefits might accrue from continued retention of equity in the target company.

We cannot begin to cover all the various arguments pro and con for cash acquisitions or define any general rule as to the desirability of tender offers. We can only observe that these offers are now a phenomenon in corporate procedures and are definitely relevant to the market decisions of those speculators who seek capital gains, or indeed to double their money quickly.

Almost without exception, an offer made by one company to purchase the stock of another will be made at a price above the prevailing quotation for the quarry's shares.

To illustrate, Unitek Corporation (a California based dental care product company) common stock ranged in price between 7½ and 18¼ on AMEX during 1975. In early 1976, it sold in the low 20's. On May 10, 1976, Airco, Inc. announced a $30 a share cash tender offer for all outstanding common shares of Unitek. This represented a total sum of $35.8 million if all Unitek shares were tendered—Unitek had sold for $22.50 as recently as April 15, 1976.

On the preceding Friday, May 7, 1976, Unitek common sold as high as 25⅞ on AMEX (up $2.75 on volume of 2,900 shares) before trading was halted on the rumor of a tender. At that time, Unitek's president, Hugo Colvin, said that the company "had no other knowledge regarding any such tender offer."

On June 15, 1976, Revlon, Inc. announced it had agreed to buy 570,000 shares of Barnes-Hind Pharmaceuticals, Inc. for $44.8 million. This followed earlier buying in that common stock, first by Cooper Laboratories, who had acquired 35 percent, and then by Syntex, which had acquired 56,200 shares at about $55. Both Cooper and Syntex bowed out, and let Revlon take over Barnes-Hind. All this was most satisfactory to earlier buyers of Barnes-Hind common, which had sold at a 1975 high of only 33¼.

On September 30, 1974, the common stock of Avis, Inc. opened at 4⅜. Later that day, it zoomed to 8⅛ on a trading volume of 20,700 shares. Why? On a rumor that Avis, Inc. shares were about to be sold by IT&T (which company then owned 52 percent and was under court order to divest its shares within a reasonable period of time). Apparently, however, somebody got wind of a deal, then in progress, to sell Avis, Inc. to UAL, Inc. and endeavored to capitalize swiftly on such privileged information. In any event, the S.E.C. suspended trading in Avis common on NYSE on the next day until the investment community could be adequately informed about what was going on.

Leaks have indeed been a recurrent problem in acquisitions and tender offers. A stenographer taking down the notes of a planned offer in a top-level executive meeting may flash the information to a friend; the clerk who Xeroxes the copies may surmise that he or she has stumbled on moneymaking information; or somebody in the firm printing up the tender offer may decide to try for a quick buck. These leaks are difficult to locate and to eliminate, and, of course, they are unfair to the great body of company stockholders who have no access to this valuable knowledge in advance.

In July, 1974, the very day before a tender of $5 a share was announced for Elba Systems Corporation, somebody who seemed to know something bought 1,500 shares at 2⅞.

Youngstown Steel Door sold as low as 8⅜ in 1974. In 1975, however, Thrall Car Manufacturing Company outlined an offer to purchase 625,000 shares of YSD at $14. Youngstown countered with a lawsuit contending that control by Thrall would violate the antitrust laws.

On Monday, May 10, 1976, Empire Gas Corporation announced an offer to purchase two million shares of the common stock of Pargas, Inc. at $18.50 a share. The stock had ranged between 8⅜ and 15⅛ in 1975 and below the tender price in early 1976.

The purpose of citing the above transactions is to alert you to a very interesting and recurrent phenomenon of the market: the opportunity to make money by early purchase of shares likely to be acquired. Almost without exception, the tender offers are at prices quite a bit higher than those for recent transactions in the subject stock, and as you have observed, the first offer is not necessarily the best nor the last. The original acquisitor may decide to better his offer in order to win over wavering shareholders, or a new suitor may come on the scene, possibly urged to action by the target company's management. A classic case of this occurred when, a decade ago, Occidental Petroleum sought to take over Kern County Land, a California company rich in oil reserves. The Kern County management wasn't happy about losing out to Occidental, so in due course Tenneco, Inc. was persuaded to buy in and take over. Tenneco did, but meanwhile Kern County shares advanced and Occidental made several million in market profit, even though it did not succeed in its takeover objective.

A man renowned for his prowess in this merger area is Victor Posner of Miami Beach, President of NVF, Inc., which, in turn, acquired, some years ago, 86 percent of Sharon Steel. In the spring of 1976, Mr. Posner was on the move again. Sharon Steel had acquired about 11 percent of the common stock of Foremost-McKesson, a $2 billion company on NYSE, and announced a plan to offer $27 face amount of Sharon Steel 8 percent bonds for each share of FOR, then trading at 16½. As expected, the Foremost management didn't like the idea and started a suit to fend off the indicated takeover. Other companies in which the Posner interests were adding to their holdings were Birnup and Sims and UV Industries, Inc.

Many times each year there will emerge tender offers for companies. Historically, these offers have almost invariably been viewed with displeasure by managements of the target companies. They usually inveigh against the acquisitors, calling their management predators, corporate raiders, market operators, or violators of antitrust laws. Even though lawsuits are initiated by the company whose shares are sought, most of these "bleats" are stilled, especially if the original tender offer is "upped" to the satisfaction of public stockholders who may be tired of their holdings anyway.

Moreover, those companies and groups, such as the Posner team, which have been quite successful in taking over companies, do a lot of analytical work in advance. They may see a company with a stodgy, entrenched executive staff, doing an inferior job in the generation or expansion of earning power. They may see that the company under study has: (1) divisions consistently unprofitable or with unsatisfactory earning power, which should be sold off; (2) rewarding markets that the company should be entering into; (3) opportunities for increased profit through better cost or inventory controls, stepped up research, rejuvenation of the sales force, or more aggressive product promotion and marketing; (4) a rich cash position with stock selling well below book value. In other words, a smart acquisition team will have some very logical reasons for wanting to bid on a particular company. The stock it proposes to buy in on, in its opinion, should be worth much more money, in due course, than the tender bid.

While forthcoming takeover plans are seldom telegraphed in advance, once they become publicly known there is usually a chance to make a profit by buying the stock below the tender price and later: (1) selling it at a higher price; (2) accepting the tender offer; or (3) benefitting from a competition wherein more than one bidder is on the scene. Under the latter condition, speculators have prospered handsomely, sometimes selling out at a price 100 percent or more above that prevailing before any tender offer had been made.

So keep your eyes open as you read the financial pages. Look for companies in which the men in management own little stock and there is a large public float. A takeover group does not need to own an absolute majority of stock. Thirty percent or so may give them control if the share ownership is widely diffused. Look also for sleepy companies in static industries where shares are languishing in the marketplace at large discounts from "book value," and particularly where they reveal a strong current asset position. Many acquisitors go after companies like this because they want to put that corporate cash to work, either to earn a better return on it or as a financial base to support still another acquisition.

Another, and usually less profit-prone type of tender is where a company decides to buy in a certain amount of its own common stock, usually because the issue is selling substantially below book value. The company has surplus cash or feels that reduction of the number of outstanding shares will permit higher per share net earnings to be reported. Another reason for this corporate cannibalism is to have a store of "treasury" stock available, if needed, to implement a merger or acquisition by tax-free exchange of securities.

For example, on May 7, 1976, Sargent-Welch Scientific Company offered to purchase 500,000 of its common shares ($1 par value) at $13 per share, reserving the right to enlarge its purchase if more than 500,000 shares were tendered. Similar "buy-in" offers were quite common during the market doldrums of 1974–75, when many issues sold at embarrassingly low prices. Companies decided to repurchase, not only to achieve the accounting benefit of buying below book value but to quiet the clamor of stockholders who protested that their stock was "doing nothing but going down!" Obviously a market order to buy several hundred thousand shares of a company's stock has a stabilizing, if not a stimulating, effect on its quotations. Several analysts have contended, however, that this buy-in procedure does not provide the best use for corporate cash. They are particularly critical of such offers, launched in order that a coterie of officers and directors may take advantage of it to "bail out" some of their own holdings (quite possibly lodged as collateral for bank loans).

Another special situation is the stock split. Rumors of stock splits have traditionally exerted a favorable influence on stock prices, and customers' brokers have repeatedly used such rumors as a sales argument to their clients. Stock splits are, indeed, a standard market device. These welcome share divisions commonly reflect substantial rises in the earnings of the subject companies and result in animated market sponsorship and endorsement of specific issues.

While stock splits are not exactly epidemic, they do occur with increasing frequency as markets gain altitude. To illustrate, in the 1974 bear market, only 27 Big Board stocks split their shares by at least 2 for 1. In 1975, the total was 32, compared with 85 in the bull market of 1972.

Random 2 for 1 splits (on listed and unlisted shares) in 1976 include:

Date	Company	Price on Date Split	Quote May 31, 1976
1/30/76	American Science & Engineering	9¾	11½
3/08/76	Carborundum	31⅜	31½
3/17/76	Continental Oil	65⅛	69¾
2/23/76	Crane Co.	75	64
2/05/76	Dow Chemical	106½	108
3/03/76	Great Northern Nekoosa	67⅞	65¼
2/17/76	Stauffer Chemical	102¼	96
1/29/76	Vulcan Materials	37¼	39⅜

From the foregoing, you will note that, after the news is out, split shares display little or no upward momentum; but in the sixty days or so before any public announcement, they may sparkle in the marketplace. To illustrate, in this two-month twilight zone before the official announcement of a split, American Science gained over 60 percent; Carborundum 20; Continental Oil (minus 5 percent); Crane Company, up 50; Dow Chemical 24; Great Northern 56; Stauffer 25; and Vulcan 12.

After the split has been implemented, a lag or "digestive" period occurs. Often, for a period of two months to six months, the new shares generally plateau in the market and do not rise beyond the top, pre-split quotation. After that, however, propellant factors take over and the corporate shares, now in a much lower price range, attract a new following and many new stockholders in a representative company.

Indeed, this is probably the dominant motivation in the management's decision to split a company's shares—to attract thousands of new shareowners by making shares available in a more popular price range. American Tel common had sold well above 100 for decades and paid a $9 dividend without interruption until, in 1974, Ma Bell decided on a 2 for 1 split. Since then, the shares have ranged between 40 and 60 and attracted millions of new owners. Telephone is now the leader in popular share ownership, with over 3,100,000 individual stockholders!

What does all this mean to you as a speculator in quest of gain? Just this—if you draw a bead on a higher-priced active stock, and conclude that it is a candidate for a split, and you buy it, the chances are you'll make a profit. Perhaps you won't double your money (although that is possible) but you may increase market value by 20 to 50 percent on your capital with a little luck.

The theory in back of all this is that middle-class Americans, who have always been the backbone of equity investment, are no longer odd-lot buyers. They want to buy "round lots" of 100 shares. Accordingly, price is an important factor. Exxon stock at around 100 was attracting, in the main, only institutional buyers. So the stock was split 2 for 1; IBM, selling currently around 260, is a stock almost everyone would like to own, but how many individuals can afford to purchase 100 shares for an outlay of $26,000? Imagine how many new owners would "come aboard" if IBM split 10 for 1 and you could buy 100 shares for $2,600!

Analysts have concluded that a 2 for 1 split can add 25 to 50 percent more stockholders within a year, and thus create a greatly expanded reservoir of capital for subsequent corporate financing, possibly via stock rights' offerings for new common, or convertible securities. Corporate managements are recognizing in increasing numbers that an army of contented share owners is a powerful corporate asset.

Further, corporate leaders, economists, and portfolio professionals are now convinced that we are not setting a proper stage for generation of the billions in new capital this country will need for its indicated future expansion. Until 1968, the number of individual stockholders had been growing steadily, but it topped out at around 31 million in 1971. Since then, the high interest rates available on top-quality bonds (8½ to 9½ percent) have lured individuals in droves away from the stock market; and in the summer of 1976, there were only 28 million stockholders. Moreover, in the period 1971–76, the average age of the individual stockholder advanced from 48 to 53. We need to reattract the younger group to the merits of stock ownership.

Institutional buying and high yield bonds are not the answer to the growth of private enterprise in America. We should launch a powerful drive for more stockholders by: (1) initiating more stock splits; (2) reducing the holding period and rate in the taxation of capital gains; and (3) reduction or elimination of dual taxation (now running about 40 percent on corporate earnings before you receive a dividend; and then personal taxation on the dividend income at your own individual bracket rate).

To achieve market gains, though probably not at the doubling level, remain on the lookout for higher priced issues that may be split, and buy them with some confidence. Whenever a stock sells regularly above 50, it's a candidate! That would include, currently, Coca-Cola, United States Steel, General Motors, Bank America, General Electric, Merck, Procter & Gamble, Getty Oil, and Johnson & Johnson. This search for possible splits can be rewarding, and if a confident market persists in 1977 there should be at least 70 such stocks in that year.

The information marshaled for this chapter is important and useful to intelligent investors. It may not highlight the best market areas in which to locate "doublers," but it can lead you to some quite predictable and quite worthwhile capital gains. Buy on the rumor and sell on the news!

Chapter XI

An Assortment of Stocks with Potentials for Doubling

This book has three main objectives: (1) to review the performance of certain issues which have doubled in past years; (2) to identify and define those qualities which outstanding market performers appear to have in common; and (3) to apply this knowledge to the selection of securities capable of major price appreciation and possible doubling in 1976–77.

It must be reemphasized that this whole idea is a bold one and that future gainful market action of the various issues depends upon a number of quite unpredictable factors: (1) the continued improvement in our economy and a bullish overall market trend in the months ahead; (2) the correctness of the expectations for above-average increase in or resumption of revenues and profits in individual companies; (3) return to a double-digit inflation in 1977; (4) no disturbing legislation in the next Presidential administration to inhibit drastically the earning power of corporations; and (5) the absence of a major armed conflict on this planet.

Within this framework, the hoped for superior performance of individual securities is based on the fundamental theory that "stock prices are the slaves of earning power"— that over a period of time the most dependable propellant to higher share prices is a substantial and continuing rise in net profits (or a restoration of profits, in the case of turnaround situations). This principle has evidenced, at times, lags and lapses. Some stocks, over extended periods, have done little or nothing marketwise in response to improvement in profits; and others, quite confusingly, have moved up rather well in the face of flat or even declining earning power. In general, however, the stellar performances in confident stock markets have been registered by companies documenting a dominant uptrend in profits. The recent performance of Houston Oil & Minerals, Rival Manufacturing, Ocean Development, Dome Petroleum, etcetera, are good illustrations.

Even though price advances within the next year may not prove to be at the rates hoped for in the issues we have cited, the bases on which the stocks were selected are still useful and may facilitate your own selection of winning stocks, months or even years after our candidates have either gained respectability or revealed their inadequacies. Further, the stocks that can double in a year must be given some leeway. What year? From the date the manuscript was finished, from the date the book was published, or the date when a particular investor got around to reading it, perhaps after a given stock had already appreciated by a fat percentage? Because of the time required between text completion and publication, we would rather judge that October 1, 1976, should be "post time" for this book, and that the stocks singled out for their presumed superiority should live up to their billings (if they are going to) by October 1, 1977, or, with a little literary license, by the end of that year. This does not mean that if or when any particular stock doubles in price, it should be instantly sold; it may still have a long way to go and prove to be a desirable long-term retention after the manner of IBM, Coca-Cola, Disney, Houston Oil & Mineral, or Schering Plough. When it comes to selling, perhaps a year from now or more, we can't very well be there to hold your hand. Here, each of you must use your own best judgment or get the best advice you can find. We had a difficult enough time winnowing hopeful stocks without the further burden of trying to name the price at which they should be sold. We'll be quite satisfied if they rise in some relationship to our expectations for them. The lowest-priced issues are the most hazardous. It is always possible that they will either go up—or blow up!

Elsewhere in the book, in special sections or categories, we have listed a number of possibly gainful shares. In this chapter, we are expanding the list without reference to their particular industries or market sectors. These various companies are, in general, thought to benefit from capable and motivated managements, adequate financing, controlled costs, satisfactory profit margins, some superiority in their particular fields, and visible uptrends in profitability. In theory, these issues are supposed to translate these corporate virtues into higher market altitudes. These stocks are expected to attract investor followings, to gain some notice in the financial press, and to generate rises in their P/E multiples at a faster rate than the increase in their net earnings. It is quite customary for the stock market to acknowledge the shares it favors by according them higher P/E multiples along with higher quotations. Our individual selections follow.

HUMANA, INC.

This company (formerly Extendicare, Inc.) is a major company in hospital ownership and management. In February, 1976, the company operated 59 general hospitals and three psychiatric hospitals with a total of 8,300 licensed beds. Most of these are located in the South; corporate headquarters are in Louisville, Kentucky. Patient care days total over 1,250,000 a year, and some 5,300 physicians are on the staffs of the various hospitals.

Humana, Inc. benefits from the economies of chain operation, especially in purchasing, accounting, cost controls, and the development of services ancillary to room and board billings. (These ancillary services now generate about 60 percent of revenues.) The chain is less dependent on Medicare and Medicaid than the general run of hospitals, and over 60 percent of its billings are defrayed by Blue Cross, insurance carriers, and direct payments. Occupancy, which was about 58 percent in 1975, is expected to improve in 1976 due to improvement in economic conditions.

Expansion of future revenues is anticipated from three new general hospitals now under construction, from a 175-bed replacement hospital in Louisville, and from a 49 percent interest (and management contract) in the 104 bed Wellington Hospital in London, England.

Revenues of HUM (NYSE stock symbol) have been in a continuous uptrend for more than a decade and advanced in fiscal 1975 (ending August 31) to $195.4 million, up from $134.67 million in fiscal 1974. In the same period, per-share net rose from $1.21 to $1.40. For the six months ending February 29, 1976, net revenues were up 44.4 percent and per-share net was 77¢, contrasted with 66¢ in the similar 1974–75 period.

In the roaring market for medical care stocks in 1969, Humana Inc. common (then Extendicare) sold at a high (adjusted for stock splits) of 39⅝. Current quotation, 14.

Gross revenues for fiscal 1976 are expected to exceed $275 million and per share net is expected at a new high (something over $1.50).

Humana, Inc. appears to be a steadily growing company and a major factor in its field, with a gross property account of $254.5 million. There is $198.0 million in long-term debt ahead of the 5,032,666 common shares outstanding, about 25 percent of which are owned by officers and directors.

Price appreciation in HUM shares might materialize in the light of the notable expansion in revenues year after year, the company's reputation for high standards of quality and operating efficiency, the large stake of management in share ownership, and the recent inauguration of cash dividends. Present indicated annual rate is 40¢, which might be increased because less cash resources will be required, due to fewer new hospitals being built. Interest expense, $13,671,000 in 1975, should be substantially lower in fiscal 1976.

HUM common has about 3,400 stockholders and the shares are held by eight institutions.

Waste Resources Corporation

This company is one of the two largest in America in waste management service. It increased its revenues by 150 percent in the four years 1972–75, and revenues and profits in 1976 were at record highs.

A serious national problem today is the disposal of solid wastes. The volume of this material is increasing alarmingly, and the answer is no longer to dump it crudely on vacant land outside of town. Waste Resources Corporation is one of the leading companies at work on the solution of this problem. It provides facilities for the collection and disposal of solid waste to commercial, residential, and industrial customers in areas of Texas, Pennsylvania, New Jersey, Missouri, California, Michigan, Ohio, Indiana and Florida. Through sixteen subsidiary corporations, it serves its customers by collecting, transporting, and disposing of solid waste and by operating landfills. The corporation is structured into three operating regions: the Western region, the Midwest region, and the Eastern region.

Waste Resources Corporation is active in technological research. In 1975 it completed facilities for a two-year study of the effectiveness of treatment of leachate (filtered liquids) from sanitary landfills under a grant from the United States Environment Protection Agency. Also, the company has completed Phase I of its resource recovery plant. This involves a system which segregates the wastes. The combustible fraction was tested in several coal firing boilers for use as a fuel supplement; and the ferrous cans were consumed at a detinning mill. Research in this area may notably increase the economy and efficiency of resource recovery and provide a new source of domestic fuel.

Waste Resources Corporation has grown rapidly, both internally and by compatible acquisitions. Two service firms were added in 1975: United Sanitation Services of Hillsborough Inc. in Tampa, Florida (the company's first operation in Florida); and Waste Services of Indiana, Inc. in Indianapolis. The company is able to generate one of the highest earnings return on revenues in the business (8.2 percent in 1975) through highly motivated profit center managers, tight financial controls, continual development of management personnel through regular training programs, and the use and good maintenance of modern equipment, including the latest designs in front- and rear-end loading trucks.

Growth. Investors following the company have been impressed by corporate growth. Revenues from continued operations, which totaled $8,715,000 in 1972, increased to $21,367,000 in 1975. Per-share net 55¢ in 1972 was 67¢ in 1975 (after a writeoff of 12¢ a share from discontinued operations). Net for the first quarter, 1976, was 22¢ a share on $5,985,000 in volume—both new highs.

At the end of 1975, there were 2,228,000 common shares outstanding following $5,314,000 in long-term debt on the balance sheet. The common trades in the OTC market under NASDAQ symbol, WASR. Current quotation is 3⅞.

This conservatively financed and ably managed company, earning 12 percent on its equity and growing steadily in an essential and expanding industrial sector, might match higher earnings with a higher P/E multiple in the months ahead.

INEXCO OIL COMPANY

Inexco looks like a company on its way. Gains in gross revenues from less than a million in 1966 to $47 million in 1975 document this.

The field of operations of Inexco is attractive. The company is aggressive in the exploration and development of oil and natural gas production and has substantial blocks of undeveloped properties. It has concentrated its activities in Louisiana, the Texas Gulf, the Rocky Mountain areas, and the mid-continent basin. Undeveloped acreage is over six million acres (3.5 million net), with some two million gross acres of permits and unexplored leases in the Northwest Territory and Yukon in Canada.

Of particular interest is a large scale uranium prospect in Saskatchewan which has enhanced market interest in the company, particularly since the June, 1976 vote in California endorsing nuclear power in that state two to one.

Net profits were in a steady uptrend until 1974, when a nonrecurring loss of $3,786,000 resulting from abandonment of certain Canadian properties reduced per-share net to a modest 8¢. Net per-share advanced to 41¢ in 1975 and should move upward in 1976.

No dividends are anticipated on the 11,778,240 shares of common outstanding because the company can profitably use its cash flow to expand oil drilling and to accelerate the development of its truly substantial uranium play in Saskatchewan. Long-term debt is about $40 million.

INX common, listed on NYSE and the Pacific Exchange, is at a stage where it could become a market favorite, now 13.

SNAP-ON TOOLS CORPORATION

The shares of this company have strong speculative appeal because of an unusual growth rate in both revenues and profits over a long period of years, plus the acknowledged leadership of Snap-On Tools Corporation in its industry.

Net sales have risen dramatically from $47.2 million in 1966 to $170.9 million in 1975, and are expected to exceed $200 million in 1976. In the same period, per-share net moved from 45¢ to $1.42. A per-share net of $2 has been estimated for 1976.

What does this company do that makes it so successful? It is the leading manufacturer of premium quality mechanics' hand tools in America, and it has developed a most successful program for the marketing of its products. The line consists of over 8,000 items, including socket wrenches, handles, open and box wrenches, screw drivers, tool chests, electronic and pneumatic tools, electronic testing and diagnostic equipment, and specially designed automotive service and repairs equipment. The company produces about two-thirds of production sold, with the balance manufactured by others to company specifications.

This diversity of products is distributed through 2,530 independent dealers who sell and deliver tools directly to mechanics from display vans. Dealers are trained in the techniques and the use of tools and assigned specific geographical areas, within which they regularly call on customers and prospects. Over 70 percent of sales are made through the dealer organization, with the remainder made to large industrial and government accounts directly by company salesmen.

Most tools are used in the repair and maintenance of motor vehicles and demand expands in almost direct ratio to total vehicles in use. As a result, yearly growth in this industry has been averaging over 7 percent.

Because of price inflation and global demand for Snap-On Tools, company sales should, in our view, move ahead about 16 percent annually, compounded until 1980. On that basis, per-share net should advance rewardingly.

There are 9.7 million shares of Snap-On Tools common outstanding, trading in the OTC market at around 32. As a growth type stock, the issue could well command a P/E multiple of 25. The cash dividend, indicated at 58¢ a share, could easily be increased. A stock split is also a possibility.

Why should SNAP (OTC trading symbol) rise in price? Because of its growth, its majority ownership by insiders, and possible exchange listing which could result in a much larger and more animate trading interest in the stock.

As an unlisted company domiciled in Kenosha, Wisconsin, SNAP up to now has not received the attention in the marketplace that it deserves. Relatively few investors are aware of its merits. With the right sponsorship, this stock could easily zoom.

OVERSEAS SHIPHOLDING GROUP, INC.

This is a major bulk shipping company operating in both the United States and world wide shipping markets. At the end of 1975, it owned and operated 46 vessels with an aggregate capacity of 4,075,100 DWT. About 635,000 DWT

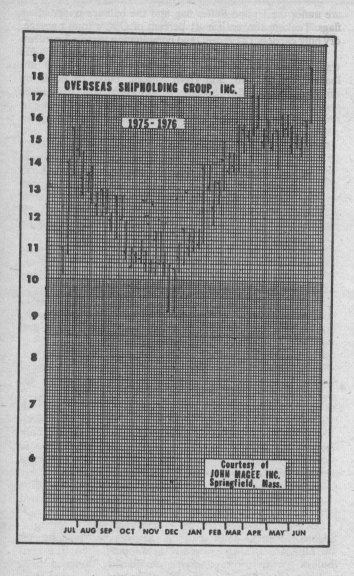

OVERSEAS SHIPHOLDING GROUP, INC.

1975 - 1976

Courtesy of
JOHN MAGEE INC.
Springfield, Mass.

are under the United States flag and the balance under other flags. Tankers account for 81 percent of OSG's total tonnage, dry bulk carriers 12 percent, and combination vessels 7 percent.

Bulk vessels are designed specifically for large volume transport of individual bulk commodities, loaded and unloaded directly into, and from, vessels, tanks or holds by on-board or shipside equipment. Tankers and dry cargo vessels embark generally on long voyages, spend little time in port, and transport one full cargo per voyage directly from point of origin to destination. Bulk carriers are contract, rather than common, carriers; and charter rates are dictated by market forces of supply and demand. Long-range planning of new building decisions are essential for success in this highly sensitive bulk shipping industry. OSG endeavors to minimize the effects of weaker periods in the charter market by long-term charters. Including new buildings, 87 percent of OSG's tonnage is chartered through 1976, and 75 percent through 1977. Company operations are sensitively tuned to demand, so that contracts have, on several occasions, been switched from tankers to dry bulk carriers, or vice versa, to provide the equipment commanding most favorable long-term charter rates at a particular time.

In the development and expansion of its business, OSG has featured a constantly growing fleet of modern vessels, long contracts with highly creditworthy charterers, and maintenance of a strong financial position.

Results over the years have been excellent. Even in 1975, when world shipping slackened and total company revenues were $156.7 million (down from $168.6 million in 1974), net profits were much higher—$3.71 a share in 1975 against $2.65 the year earlier. For the three months ending March 31, 1976, net income was $9,623,100, or 95¢ a share, contrasted with $6,886,558, or 68¢ a share, in the corresponding 1975 period. In the first quarter, 1976, a new 80,250 deadweight ton tanker was added to the fleet and placed in charter until the end of 1978.

There are 9,750,430 common shares of OSG outstanding listed on NYSE and trading at around 19, with an indicated 20¢ dividend. Long-term debt is $208.7 million.

OSG common appears as a desirable equity for gain-oriented investors because of the capability of management, the high annual percentage of vessel operations, the continuing growth of an efficient, functionally designed fleet, and the durability of global petroleum and dry cargo shipping markets. Whether in carrying oil from the North Slope, grain to Russia, or natural gas from Algeria, OSG has the equipment, the navigational skills, and able crews to perform effectively and to maintain its profitability against formidable competition.

HAMILTON BROTHERS PETROLEUM

This OTC company is interesting because it was the first producer in the North Sea and has been a pioneer in the design and construction of offshore floating systems for petroleum production. In early 1976, an affiliate, Hamilton Brothers Oil Company of Denver, entered a joint venture with Sedco for constructing and operating sophisticated floating production for clients, world wide.

Hamilton's production is on the rise. For 1975, total oil and gas sales rose from $17.2 million (1974) to $28.9 million, with earnings advancing on a per share basis from $1.36 to $1.80 a share. A considerable portion of Hamilton's production is in Canada, and the company set up for 1975 a contingent liability for possible application of Canadian income taxes. The company believes it is entitled to the benefits of the United States-Canada tax treaty which would allow Hamilton to deduct provincial royalties paid on production.

Over all, the Hamilton Brothers picture is attractive. North Sea production is now running 30,000 barrels a day, Canadian production is increasing, the company has interests in nine separate tracts on the North Slope and in domestic exploration in the Rocky Mountain and West Texas areas, as well as in offshore California and Louisiana areas.

There are 6,302,000 shares of Hamilton Brothers Petroleum common outstanding, trading under OTC symbol HAML. The stock sold at 47¾ some years ago, when its earnings were far less attractive and defined. No dividends are anticipated because the company likes to plow back profits. A stock designed for capital gains and with good prospects for realizing them; quoted at 21 at this writing.

CONTROL DATA CORPORATION

In the era when computer shares were the market darlings, Control Data Corporation was a highly visible virtuoso.

Its common stock reached an all-time high of 163½. In 1974, however, earnings plummeted from $3.40 a share (1973) to a deficit of 22¢ a share. Market quotation reflected this sharp transition from a steady rise in profits over several years to a loss; and CDA (NYSE symbol for the common stock) hit a 1974 low of 9½.

In our view, however, Control Data is staging a strong recovery that should, in due course, cause the memory of 1974 to fade in the minds of investors and generate a renewed market confidence and higher prices for CDA common. Fundamental changes in corporate operations are building a new base for earning power and reducing some of the risks that eroded profits in 1974.

By any standards Control Data is a corporation of stature. It ranks as (1) the world leader in the supply of computer services; (2) the leading manufacturer of original equipment and plug compatible peripherals; and (3) an important factor in the production of large-scale computer systems.

Important in any consideration of CDA is its transition from a company heavily involved in the specialized manufacture of large computer systems to a service company featuring effective combinations of hardware, software and data services, increasing the productivity of computer installations. Data service is a substantial sub-market in the industry, growing in annual volume from $1.3 billion in 1970 to $3 billion this year, and expected to reach $7 billion in 1980. CDA is the largest factor in this field—an area IBM is enjoined from entering until 1979. By then, CDA should be solidly entrenched. New entrants are unlikely because of the heavy investment in hardware required and the sophisticated expertise needed to keep abreast of rapid technological progress.

Control Data will remain a significant factor in the large computer systems market with its latest CYBER 170 series, acclaimed for its excellence in scientific and engineering fields, and marketed world wide. Control Data also features a 38,500 Mass Storage System, giving instant access to a sizable library of tape cartridges at far less cost than existing systems and a new family of small computers that CYBER 18 recently introduced.

In 1975, CDA had total revenues of $1,246 million, of which 51 percent represented rental and service revenues (up from 35 percent in 1970). After a $52 million writeoff of expenses in 1974, Control Data cleared the decks for resurgent profitability in computer operations in 1975 and 1976 and for greater stability of revenue flow than in the past.

Commercial Credit Company. Control Data also has a very large, wholly owned but unconsolidated subsidiary, Commercial Credit Company, which has actually provided most of the profits of Control Data for the past five years. Commercial Credit is an impressive financial service company providing both corporate and consumer financing, with receivables at December 31, 1975, of over $4 billion. In addition to personal and business loans and installment financing, Commercial Credit is in leasing and in real estate financing. It is also in life, accident-and-health, credit, and property insurance. Commercial Credit contributed $28.4 million to Control Data earnings in 1975. This was lower than in 1974 because its insurance operations, Calvert/Cavalier, the casualty subsidiary, had a pre-tax loss of $20.8 million in 1975. Certain writedowns of insurance operations, taken in 1975, are not recurring losses and should really have been taken in earlier years. However that may be, Commercial Credit operations are expected to improve in 1976 and to contribute around $35 million to CDA.

At 3/31/76, Control Data had long-term liabilities of $370.4 million and debt had been reduced by $84 million in 1975. Capitalization was $37.1 million in preferred stock and 15.9 million shares of common. Book value was about $51 a share.

It seems reasonable to expect CDA's per-share net for 1976 in the range of $2.65, a respectable gain over $2.16 in 1975. Moreover, the shares may begin to win back their one-time glamour, and command a multiple higher than 11 (at the current quote of 24). Control Data may be a sleeper.

MITCHELL ENERGY AND DEVELOPMENT CORPORATION

This company has been bracketed by some analysts with Houston Oil and Minerals because, like Houston, it has been active in oil and gas exploration off the Texas Gulf Coast. Through subsidiaries, MND (symbol for the common stock on AMEX) has been successfully exploring for and producing oil and natural gas on land in North Texas and in the Gulf.

As of January 31, 1976, MND had proved reserves of approximately 14.6 million barrels of oil and some 410 billion cubic feet of gas. Both production and reserves have been increasing. In addition, the company has twenty gas processing plants and a gas gathering and transport system with an 875-mile pipeline serving thirteen counties in North Texas.

MND also has important real estate holdings, about 65,000 acres, located for the most part in the Houston area. Long-term corporate planning involves the sale of a large part of the real estate in due course, keeping, however, a new community development known as Woodlands, covering some 20,000 acres in an area north of Houston.

The romance in MND is found in well completions and an important oil field discovery in the offshore Gulf near Galveston (the same general area where Houston Oil has been so fortunate). The corporation, in June of 1976, announced an increase in the current year's budget for offshore and bay oil exploration and drilling to $45 million (from $33 million originally planned).

Capitalization, apart from about $132 million in real estate liabilities, consists of $82.6 million in long-term debt followed by 6,490,430 common shares, quoted currently at 33. A 10¢ cash dividend was inaugurated in January, 1976. The stock is closely held. With more good fortune offshore, the shares could double within a reasonable period of time. (Since this was written, there has been a 25 percent stock dividend paid.)

SOLA BASIC INDUSTRIES

The business of Sola Basic began in 1867 and grew, under the name of Froedert Grain and Malting Company, to be a major supplier of barley malt to the brewing industry. In the 1950's, however, the company started a diversification into electrical equipment through the acquisition of Sola Electric. In 1965, the company's traditional business in malting and grain was sold off.

Today, after a series of acquisitions over the past 17 years, Sola Basic Industries, Inc. devotes its efforts exclusively to the manufacture and marketing of electric and electronic equipment through a dozen divisions, thirteen well-regarded brand names, and a line including over 2,500 assorted products and systems used in the distribution, control and application of electric power.

The company serves four major markets: electric utilities (18 percent); communications utilities (16 percent); electrical construction and industrial production (33 percent each). The company's operations are international in scope, with 20 percent of overall 1976 sales (fiscal year ending March 31, 1976) derived from foreign countries. Sales abroad are generated through four companies in Japan and individual marketing companies in Canada, Colombia, Mexico, Puerto Rico, Spain, Australia, and Hong Kong. Domestic distribution involves the services of over 75 field salesmen and some 400 independent sales "reps."

Important in the expansion and profitability of Sola is its increasing penetration of the fast-growing semi-conductor industry. In 1976, Sola acquired Unicorp, Inc., and Corotek Corporation, both identified with the development and production of equipment for semi-conductor manufacturers. More traditional products include transformers, electrical equipment for special uses—offshore drilling and computer centers—and wiring, fitting, and insulating devices and materials, heat process and microelectronic equipment.

Growth. Well-planned growth on a long-term basis has led to rising sales, profit margins and net income. In fiscal 1976, results reflected the recession, and sales fell from the historic high of $168.8 million, recorded in 1975, to $152.2 million in 1976. By effective cost controls and better capital utilization, however, net profits reached an all-time high of $7.3 million in fiscal 1976, equal to $2.12 a share on 3,400,000 common shares, versus $2.06 the year earlier. Profit margins, 7.7 percent in 1975, were increased in 8.8 percent a year later.

Sola Basic draws rather heavily in its business on new capital construction. Rising outlays in this economic sector have favored the company in 1976, and increased its business backlog by $4.5 million in the last quarter of the fiscal year recently ended. Ahead, the company looks forward to sales gains in its more traditional lines and significant progress in the semi-conductor area.

Sola Basic has paid continuous dividends for 41 consecutive years. The present dividend, now 80¢, has been increased four times in the past 3½ years. Company policy is to pay out about 33 percent of net profits in cash dividends.

For fiscal 1977, the projection is for sales above $185 million and a per share net in the order of $2.75 or $2.80.

On this basis, Sola Basic's shares are reasonably priced at around 17 (at about six times indicated current earnings and well below the $20.25 book value of the common at 3/31/76). Current cash position is strong, and there is only $18,704,000 in long-term debt. This issue could move up briskly with a little more market sponsorship.

BUTTES GAS & OIL COMPANY

Buttes Gas & Oil, with headquarters in Oakland, California, is moving forward at a lively pace in three areas: (1) oil and natural gas exploration and production and dealing in oil and gas leases; (2) contract drilling; and (3) agricultural products (mainly nuts, grapes, and citrus fruits) in three states.

BGO has considerable romance due to its sizable interests in petroleum prone real estate. This is located in sixteen states, in Canada, and off-shore at Abu Musa Island in the Persian Gulf. There are also mineral rights in six states and in Mexico. Of the mineral claims, the most promising is a prospect in Colorado believed to contain over 400 million tons of commercial grade titanium ore. In nonproducing oil land Buttes has interests in about 679,130 gross acres in the United States and in 14,695,715 acres elsewhere.

Contract drilling accounted for about 44 percent of revenues in 1975 from highly utilized operation of 45 rigs in the United States and one abroad.

Apparently the Persian Gulf wells are rich producers. Crude from that area and from the United States, plus natural gas production in Canada and the United States (about 4,800,000 MCF in 1975), are expected to increase in 1976 and another new high in operating revenues is anticipated. Revenues increased 45 percent in 1975 to $104.5 million. Earnings per-share were $3.54 with 4,151,286 shares outstanding (symbol BGO). There is long-term debt of $124.3 million, including $9,750,000 of subordinated 5½ percent debentures due 1988 and convertible each into 42.9 shares. These are also attractive.

Buttes has had a couple of lawsuits over the Abu Musa concession, one which it won against Occidental Petroleum (but the decision is to be appealed); and another one by Clayco Petroleum, unresolved.

The expectation for speculative animation in the case of Buttes stems from: (1) the panoramic spread of its petroleum and mineral interests; (2) the upward trend in oil and gas prices; and (3) the steeply rising curve of revenues and a jump in per share net from 7¢ in 1970 to $3.54 (primary) in 1976. The company earned 26 percent on stockholders' equity in 1975, which is excellent! Buttes will be a volatile performer and has the ingredients for market ascent. The stock is at this time quoted at 21½.

PALM BEACH COMPANY

This widely known company first gained consumer acceptance with its line of men's light fabric suits for summer or tropical wear. With the passage of years, the company broadened out and now carries a complete line of men's and boys' tailored apparel for year-round use, tuxedos, coats and slacks for sportswear, plus women's tailored clothing, sports and swimwear and coordinates. Brand names for men include: Palm Beach, Royal Palm Beach, John Weitz, and Springweave; and for women, Craig Craely, Austin-Hill, and Evans-Picone. For the year ending October 31, 1975, business volume was distributed as follows: 77 percent men's wear, 4 percent boys' wear, and 19 percent women's wear. The masculine line is marketed through more than 4,500 specialty clothing and departments stores nationwide.

The economic recovery of 1975–76, stimulating a boom in consumer spending that will helpfully continue through 1977, would appear to favor this company because of the moderate prices of its products, its reputation for quality, and the aggressive advertising of its brand names. Relatively low-cost production is made possible by location of a great portion of plant and warehouse facilities in the South. A modest amount of direct selling is done through three owned menswear outlets in Honolulu, Salt Lake City, and New Haven.

Growth of PMB has been steady but not explosive, with sales increasing in every year in the past decade except 1974. The net sales total in fiscal 1975 was $117.7 million, up from $34.5 million in 1966. Per-share net averaged about $1.04 for the past three years but may move to new high ground in 1976 due to: (1) improved cost controls; (2) higher profit margins as costs are spread over larger number of units produced; (3) reduction of interest charges; (4) licensing of pro-

duction and sales of Palm Beach brands with a subs
company in Japan to serve that country and the Far
and with a significant Canadian company to expand the ꞔa-
nadian market; (5) possible acquisitions; and (6) the increasing consumer demand for larger, more stylish, and colorful
wardrobes.

Capitalization is quite leveraged with 2,845,692 common
shares preceded on the balance sheet by $18.9 million in long-
term debt. PMB (NYSE symbol) sold at 25¾ in 1969
when it was a much inferior stock. Current dividend is 30¢,
which might be increased. PMB is a low-priced cyclical issue
that could move up sharply in an animated market. Currently
at 7⅝.

COMTECH LABORATORIES

Comtech Laboratories is a scientific company that has
moved well past the pure research stage and is now attractive
as a growth-type stock rapidly expanding its earning power. To
illustrate, net sales for the fiscal year ending July 31, 1975,
were $16,560,000, a 60 percent gain over the preceding year;
and in the same period net profits more than doubled from
45¢ to 94¢.

Comtech is a specialist in the design, construction and installation of satellite communication earth stations, including
systems for receiving and transmitting and for sophisticated
digital communication equipment. Customers include telephone and telegraph companies, common carriers, companies
and contractors engaged in space communication, as well as
the United States and other governments.

This is not a business of standard hardware. Most sales are
made through competitive bidding whether on complete stations or on systems or subsystems, on fixed price contracts.
A complete receiving and transmission system may cost up
to $1 million, and a fully equipped earth station, ready to
operate, four times that.

Because of the size of these contracts and the length of
time required to complete them, the company has need for
bank finance. This is being taken care of through a $10 mil-
lion line of credit arranged in 1975 with interest rates at
½ percent over prime.

Comtech has recently built a new 123,000 square foot
plant adjoining its original facility in Smithtown, New York,

about half as large as the main plant. While not a major factor in its industry, Comtech Laboratories has displayed a vigor and competence of management, as well as research and innovative talents, that have kept the company competitive and increasingly profitable in a highly sophisticated industry.

Comtech has 1,601,140 common shares outstanding and $700,370 in long-term debt. The common stock trades in the OTC market under the symbol, CMTL. About 20 per cent of the common is held by management. The shares pay no dividend. This is a growth situation with sales doubling in the six-month period ending January 31, 1976, and net tripling from 25¢ a share in the same 1975 period to 76¢. The issue appears attractive on its own, or as a possible merger candidate. It is currently at 15½.

AFFILIATED HOSPITAL PRODUCTS, INC.

This unusual company in the medical care industry specializes in disposable hospital products and in medical furniture. Affiliated Hospital Products is composed of three distinct manufacturing and marketing groups: the Perry Group, the Equipment Group, and MPL, Inc.

The Perry Group is a leading supplier of disposable items for hospitals and physicians, such as surgeons' and examination gloves, Perry Foley catheters, and catheter kits. These are sold domestically and overseas, with volume in Europe and Latin America generating 12 percent of 1975 sales. Perry latex gloves have a reputation for top quality and are found in doctors' offices and hospital surgeries world wide.

The Equipment Group features medical furniture marketed under Shampaine, Carrom, and Wilson brand names. The line includes the Carrom electric hospital bed, the Mark V motorized examination table, the Radi-Op surgical table for radio-graphic assisted surgery, patient and examining room tables and furniture, and the Wilson line of stainless steel hospital equipment. Siemens-Elema of Sweden now distributes the Radi-Op line in several foreign countries.

MPL, Inc. is a manufacturer of disposable needles for medical, dental, hospital and laboratory use. Featured are Quick-Draw blood collecting needles that insure against leakage. The SoloPak unit drug delivery system is quite successful and has been extensively promoted in hospital pharmacies and respiratory therapy departments. A new 310,000 square foot facility was acquired in Franklin Park, Illinois to produce SoloPak. Sales in the United States are generated through several hundred medical supply distributors, on a nonexclusive basis, supplementing company salesmen.

Affiliated Hospital Products is headquartered in St. Louis, Missouri and has over 1,800 employees. The company was incorporated in Delaware in 1965 and formed by amalgamation of two subsidiaries of United Industrial Corporation, which remains the largest holder of AFH common (traded on AMEX under that symbol) with approximately 63 percent ownership.

AFH common sold as high as 40 in 1968. Current quotation, at around $8 a share, reflects 1975 sales, which rose only 4 percent over 1974 to $38.4 million. Per-share net last year nevertheless advanced nicely to $1.07 from 42¢ a year earlier. (The 1974 figures were penalized, however, by a switchover to LIFO inventory valuation.)

AFH is conservatively capitalized with $4 million in long-term debt ahead of 1,765,893 shares of common held by about 2,500 shareowners. Return on net worth was about 15 percent in 1975. The financial position is good with a 2½ to one current ratio.

Indications are for continuing gains in sales and profits in 1976 and a possible increase in dividends, now at 32¢ a year. AFH is in an industry that, in the past, has carried a glamour rating. A significant advance in per-share net during 1976 and on into 1977 might well justify a much higher market price for this stock.

ROCKET RESEARCH CORPORATION

This sophisticated technology company is currently attracting attention not so much for its rocketry as for a sealant material that seals punctures automatically and might make spare tires unnecessary.

Rocket Research Corporation has been a significant factor in the research, development, and production of space hardware, with a flawless record of performance in a number of the key United States space programs during the past year. These have included NASA Earth Resources Technology Satellite (LANDSAT), Synchronous Meteorological Satellite (SMS), Geocentrical Orbiting Environmental System (GOES) and Applications Technology Satellite (ATS), plus programs for the Department of Defense.

Exotic as these activities sound, however, investor interest in Rocket Research Corporation now centers on an intensely practical proprietary product with an exciting global market potential—a material that seals punctures in tires at temperatures up to 270 degrees and at speeds up to 100 miles an hour. After development over a three-year period and extensive testing, this sealant has now gained significant acceptance. Fleet tests indicate that the RRC sealant (tires are coated with it on the inside) eliminates 80 per cent of the tread puncture flat-tire problems normally occurring on passenger automobiles. The sealant remains in place, performs under severe conditions of road stress, and retains its effectiveness as a puncture sealant for the life of the tire.

While technological breakthroughs such as this are always of interest, the acid test is the conversion of the proprietary items into corporate profits. In this case, the prospects for profitability appear excellent. On December 10, 1975, Uniroyal Tire Company ordered equipment to coat Uniroyal tires. The first system, a tire sealant continuous-applicator machine, was shipped to Uniroyal in March, 1976.

In addition to supplying Uniroyal with both sealant and application equipment, Rocket Research has licensed Yokohama Rubber Company, second largest tire producer in Japan, to use its sealants in their tires. Yokohama has also purchased a continuous application system, as well as a Rocket engineered tire cleaning machine.

The self-sealing tire represents a major advance in motor travel because it may eliminate spare tires on cars and trucks, long a top-priority goal of the motor industry. It obviously opens up broad horizons for expansion of sales and profits at RRC.

Rocket Research, operating through a series of corporate divisions, is a leading manufacturer of monopropellant guidance and attitude control rocket engines, gas generators, pulsed high voltage systems and explosives systems for the stimulation of oil and gas wells. Larse Corporation, a company specializing in telecommunication equipment and 69.3 percent owned by RRC is scheduled to become fully owned through a merger agreement recently announced calling for an exchange of shares—two shares of RRC for each share of the remaining 30.7 percent minority interest in Larse Corporation.

Another subsidiary, Physics International Company of San Leandro, California, acquired in 1975, has been a leader in research in the application of electron beam technology to fusion processes. The objective of this research is the eventual development of controlled thermonuclear reactors, generally considered to be the ultimate future energy source.

Physics International is to supply a large electrical capacitor system for the Doublet III fusion research project of General Atomic Company, a part of ERDA's national program to apply nuclear fission to power production. PI has also gained wide recognition for its research in piezoelectric technology. Piezoelectricity is a phenomenon in which certain materials expand and contract precisely under the application of voltage. The principle has already been effectively applied by PI to a fuel injection system for diesel engines, in partnership with CAV, Ltd. of England. PI received in January, 1976, second year funding on a $560,000 two-year contract with National Institutes of Health for the development of an implantable heart-assist system centering around a piezoelectric "pump" to synchronize physiological variations in pulse and blood flow rates.

Other RRC output includes proprietary inflation devices for automobile air cushion restraint systems and a new patented method for mass producing electronic printed circuit boards. In fact, we could not begin in limited space to cover all the facets of RRC activities. The company evidences a broad gauged technological competence and is steadily converting its research efforts into marketable products.

For fiscal 1975 (year ends October 31), the company reported total revenues of $17,080,000 and net earnings of 27¢ a share on 2,959,303 shares outstanding. This was below the per-share net of 41¢ reported a year earlier (although 1975 sales were higher by $1.2 million), due in part to discontinuance of certain unprofitable activities.

Rocket Research Corporation common stock trades OTC at around $5½. It is a glamour stock with visible prospects for forward motion. It benefits from an able management team and a prestigious board of directors.

THE CYCLOTRON CORPORATION

Cyclotron is a sophisticated company in the scientific field; its headquarters are in Berkeley, California, and it is engaged in the design and manufacture of compact cyclotrons and other accelerator systems, including equipment used in cancer therapy, nuclear medical systems and physics research.

A cyclotron is an orbital particle accelerator used for accelerating positive ions. Once accelerated, these ions are applied to bombard target nuclei, which then produce radioisotopes and fast neutrons. Certain of these radioactive isotopes are useful in nuclear medicine, while the fast neutrons are now used in neutron therapy. About 45 percent of the 1975 company revenues were generated by cyclotron sales.

Sales are made primarily to hospitals, research and scientific institutions, universities, nuclear process companies, and government agencies, domestically and in many foreign nations—Germany, Saudi Arabia, England, Scotland, Brazil.

In common with most scientific and research enterprises, Cyclotron required considerable time to convert its laboratory progress into profitability; and for the years 1971 through 1974, the company operated at a loss. In 1975, however, the company made a bottom-line breakthrough. It increased its sales from $1,918,000 in 1974 to $2,840,000 in 1975, and reported a per-share net of $1.04 in that year (against a 66¢ a share deficit in 1974).

The capital structure at 12/31/75 was $183,293 in long-term debt followed by 274,000 common shares. This stock was split 2 for 1 in April, 1976, and there are approximately 1,400 share owners (with 25 percent owned by management). The stock trades in the OTC market around 9, with a NASDAQ trading symbol CYCC.

In view of the broadening international acceptance of neutron therapy, and the company's documented capability in effective cyclotron and neutron equipment, CYCC common may now be in line for rapid enhancement in corporate stature and profitability.

ATLAS CORPORATION

Atlas Corporation shares are selected for gain because of the historic dedication of this company to uranium, and the rather bright prospects of this mineral in the long-term solution of the United States fuel shortage.

Uranium mining and processing is centered at Moab, Utah where Atlas processes uranium ore, and from which point it has contracts to deliver 2.9 million pounds of uranium concentrate through 1980. Natural resource revenues (principally uranium) generated about 46 percent of income before taxes in fiscal 1975 (fiscal year ending June 30, 1975).

Atlas also has four divisions devoted to manufacturing: Titleflex, maker of flexible metal tubes and hoses for aero industries; Western Sky Industries, manufacturer of metal and automotive and aircraft plastic products; Camden Lime Co., Central mixed and precast concrete, plus mason supplies; and Brocton Sole & Plastics, featuring leather, rubber, and polyethylene materials used in shoes and sporting goods. There is also International Atlas Services, which operates a joint venture, Global Associates (55 percent owned) providing special services for NASA, the United States Army and Air Force, and which manages Atlas's (80 percent owned) Indian Pacific operations.

Over the past three years, net sales have expanded from $38.3 million (1973) to $51.8 million in fiscal 1975; and in 1975 per share net rose moderately to 11¢ from 7¢ the year earlier. For the first six months of fiscal 1976, net income totaled 20¢ a share. Net sales for the full year were expected to exceed $58 million.

Long-term debt is $2,745,559, followed by 38,283 shares of $20 par $1 preferred stock, and 14,775,384 shares of common quoted at around 4¼. There are also outstanding 5 million perpetual warrants to buy AZ common at $6.25. Both the warrants (quoted at 2) and the common are listed on AMEX. The big speculative kick here is in the rising price (and demand) for U_3O_8 concentrate, of which Atlas has a good supply.

UNITED SERVICES LIFE COMPANIES

United Services Life Insurance, although a parent of five subsidiary companies, retains its identity as a medium-sized stock life insurance company with over $260 million in assets and over $2.7 billion of life insurance in force. Organized in 1937, USLC specializes in insuring military officers and their families. In this field, United Services has built up a highly successful and steadily growing institution, returning 18.5 percent on its stockholders' equity in 1975.

Growth is evidenced by expansion of life insurance in force from $1.8 billion, in 1971, to $2.78 billion in 1975. Of that amount, $1.68 billion was in whole life and endowment

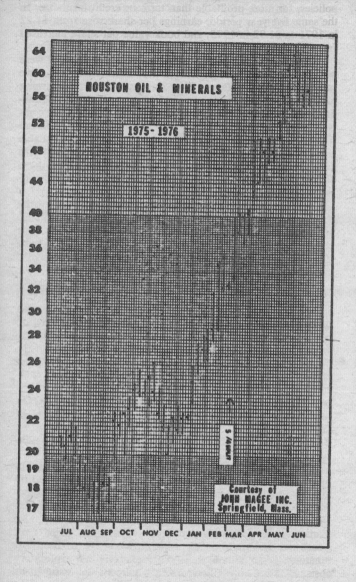

policies, far more profitable than term or credit insurance. In the same five-year period, earnings per-share rose from $1.22 in 1971 to $1.92 in 1975; and book value per share increased from $7.26 to $11.60.

In the 1950's and early 1960's, life insurance stocks were popular and sold at high P/E ratios. Since then they have rather fallen out of favor. They now appear to be returning to market vogue with such issues as Kansas City Life, Franklin, and Connecticut General performing well. Statistical comparison with such well-entrenched life companies would seem to favor United Services, because its shares are now available (around 9½ OTC) at below book value—and at roughly five times indicated 1976 earnings of above $2 a share, paying a 40¢ dividend. Invested assets of $250 million earned 6.75 gross for United Services in 1975.

This issue, with 2,715,000 shares outstanding, may not be an active daily trader, but its unusual earning power should, in due course, be reflected in substantially higher prices. And the company might be sought as a desirable acquisition.

HOUSTON OIL & MINERALS

Houston Oil & Minerals Corporation (HOI on AMEX) has an impressive record of aggressive management, outstanding drilling success, and rapidly rising gas reserves, with an unusual rate of growth in net profits and cash flow.

HOI has concentrated on offshore drilling for gas and oil near Galveston, Texas, and in the Gulf of Mexico. The company discovered the Bolivar Field and developed it with extension wells to an estimated production of about 225 MM cubic feet per day by the end of 1976 (up from 180 MM in 1975). The Bolivar Field now provides about 98 percent of HOI gas production and roughly 30 percent of oil and condensation.

Earnings from Bolivar alone would make HOI an attractive stock, but company prospects are further brightened by extensive drilling in the areas of other, more recent discoveries: Shipwreck (apparently the most promising), Texas City Dike, Half Moon Shoal and Dollar Points Fields. Long-range plans call for continued exploration along the Texas Gulf Coast and offshore in the Gulf of Mexico. HOI has been fortunate in locating major fields with relatively low exploratory costs. HOI has so far been over 50 percent successful in its wildcat drillings in the Galveston Bay area, and is expected to drill approximately 48 wildcats in 1976, with $130 million budgeted for exploration and development drilling this year. Looking ahead, HOI has some 312,000 net acres in the Rocky Mountains and has already started wildcat drilling there.

Significant in the profitability of HOI are attractive intrastate prices for gas. To illustrate, the company has recently signed a ten-year contract (80 percent take or pay) with United Texas Transmission Company for sale of gas at $1.95 per MM BTU (with transportation costs by the company's pipeline subsidiary added). Initial deliveries at 125 MMCF/D are expected to begin in February or March of 1977. This gas is to be supplied by the new Shipwreck Fields. This contract alone may increase annual company revenues by as much as $65 million.

Capitalization of HOI is $119,610,000 in long-term debt (including an outstanding issue of approximately $26 million of 6¼ percent debentures convertible into common at $19.20 a share), 47,659 shares of $1 par preferred stock, and 8,100,000 shares of common. The common is expected to earn about $4.50 a share in 1976, and over $7 in 1977. Current indicated dividend is 80¢; the stock was split 4 for 3 in 1972, 2 for 1 in 1973 and 1974, and 5 for 4 in 1976.

A volatile performer, ranging as high as 70 in 1976 and now trading at 68, it should do well as a rapidly expanding energy producer in a period of insistent demand for fossil fuels.

To wind up this section of the book, here are three "quickies"—quickies only in the sense that we are mentioning them briefly—that you may find worthy of investigation and investment: (1) Land Resources common, a low-priced realty speculation (1⅝ OTC); (2) Earth Resources (15 on Amex), a company with a Mid-South refinery and gas stations, an Alaskan construction company, the North Pole Refinery coming up, and a promising Idaho silver mine; (3) Kagot, Inc. (about 9 OTC) a recreational products company (travel trailers, pontoon boats and especially Gentronics CB Radios); and (4) Westbury Resources, busy acquiring coal assets (OTC, 2½).

Chapter XII

Canadian Investment Opportunities

In the great bull market of the 1920's, American investors took relatively small interest in investments outside the United States. While common stocks, such as United Fruit (now United Brands), with ownership of extensive properties in the banana plantations of Central America—along with International Nickel, world leader in nickel with its principal properties in Canada; International Tel. & Tel., holding telephone utilities in several nations; American & Foreign Power and Canadian Pacific Railroad, plus others—were all popular on Wall Street, they represented but a very small fraction of total American investments.

Investment abroad was stimulated, toward the end of the 1920's, by public offering in the United States of high yielding foreign bonds: Italy 7's, Belgium 7½'s, Argentine 6's, Cologne 6½'s, Bolivia 8's, San Salvador 8's, Chile 6's, etc. In the 1920's, over $400 million in foreign bonds were publicly offered in the United States. Investors were motivated to purchase them by (1) high interest returns offered, (b) by confidence in world peace, and (3) by the enthusiastic recommendation of bond salesmen. The later market history of these offerings did little to popularize overseas investment because, within a decade, more than 70 per cent of these various foreign bond issues were in default.

Of all the foreign nations of the world, Canada has been the favorite haven for American investment. That country is most similar to the United States. We have many attributes in common—the living style in metropolitan cities, the devotion to democratic government and to an enterprise economy, the rising living standards, and the broad unionization of labor are just a few of our common characteristics.

Canada has a land area 20 percent larger than that of the United States but has only one-tenth of our population, clustered for the most part within 150 miles of the Canadian-American border. The investment appeal of Canada has been provided by its fabulous store of natural resources—vast forests, rich underground stores of minerals, abundant petroleum and water power, fine inland and ocean ports, ocean fishing, and millions of acres of wheatlands on the Western prairies. Over the years, these immense natural resources have required large inputs of capital for their development and exploitation. A major portion of this capital, often representing control of Canadian corporations, has been supplied year after year by the United States—so much so that, particularly in the last decade, opposition to American domination of Canadian companies has become a national political issue. Definite steps have been taken to discourage and to reduce American penetration of Canadian industry. For one thing, there is a tax on dividends on Canadian shares held by foreigners. With respect to any substantial new investment from abroad, or an attempt to take over the control of a Canadian company, the matter comes quickly under the surveillance of the Foreign Investment Review Agency. On several occasions, this agency has rejected American bids to take over Canadian industrial properties, even when they might clearly benefit the Canadian economy. American direct investment in Canada, formerly at the rate of about $1 billion a year, is now half that.

Not only have measures been taken at various levels of government, provincial and dominion, to limit and control foreign capital, but recent economic initiatives within Canada have been veering toward socialism, at least in the opinion of many observers. Corporate dividends have been frozen temporarily; profits may not exceed 85 percent of a defined base period, although wages and salaries may be increased ten per cent annually (possibly more). Further, capital investment in the Dominion has become far less attractive and rewarding than in earlier years. For example, in 1963, Canadian wages were 26.2 percent below United States wages. In May, 1976, however, the average hourly wage for Canadian workers in manufacturing was $5.21—higher than the $4.98 figure in the United States.

Until the recent application of wage and price controls, there was indeed little restraint on union wages. Canadian workers across the board gained 16.8 percent in annual increases in union wage contracts concluded in 1975 versus 7.8 per cent in the United States. Even wage controls seem to have provided only a moderate braking effect, with contracts concluded in the first six months of 1976 averaging 14 percent higher annually.

It costs over $10,000 a year for a family of four to live moderately in Canada; and the price of single family houses has doubled in the past five years. Thus, as in the United States, it has become almost impossible for young couples in Canada to buy their own homes.

Not only at the Dominion level, but regionally, there are evidences of the advance of socialism in Canada. British Columbia has increased the taxation of mining companies, and so has Quebec. In Saskatchewan, there has been a government takeover of potash properties. The political climate there is discouraging, if not hostile, to traditional capitalistic development of commerce and industry.

Canadian unemployment has been running at about 7 percent; with inflation at 9 percent in 1976. In the maritime provinces—Nova Scotia, New Brunswick and Newfoundland —conditions remain seriously depressed, with unemployment in certain sections running as high as 40 percent.

In late 1974, Prime Minister Trudeau thought that drastic steps were required to defend Canada against a recession that was rapidly moving across the Western World. He sponsored expansive fiscal and monetary policies and introduced the wage and price controls cited earlier. However desirable these steps may have seemed at the time, they have not achieved the economic corrections sought. Inflation appears headed for double digits, output per hour in industry has declined, and exports, which normally account for 20 percent of Canada's Gross National Product, have been declining. (The Taiwan fiasco at the Montreal Olympics highlighted Trudeau's desperate efforts to obtain a more favorable balance of trade through continued export of wheat to mainland China.)

Canada seems to be pricing itself out of many world markets and reported a record trade deficit of $5.5 billion in 1975. Newsprint, a major export item, is on the downturn due to strikes and price increases, with sales to the United States now running at a 5.5 million ton annual rate, down from 6.9 million tons in 1974.

Monetary experts seem to think the Canadian dollar is too high when at a premium over the United States dollar. They believe it would be better (and would definitely enhance Canadian exports) if the Canadian dollar went to a discount. Another whopping trade deficit in 1976 might depreciate the Canadian dollar and make the country's products thus more attractive in export markets.

While the foregoing capsuled description of the Canadian economy paints a rather negative picture for American investors, the political climate, in Canada, as in the United States, can change quite dramatically within a relatively short period of time. In British Columbia, for example, David Barrett was elected Premier in 1974. He introduced a number of quite radical Socialist measures, raising the taxes on the mining and petroleum industries and placing new restrictions on security transactions within the Province. In 1975, however, Premier Barrett was ousted and replaced by a candidate whose economic views are more moderate. Some of the more drastic legislation of the Barrett administration has already been repealed, and there is a general feeling that the political pendulum is swinging back toward the economic philosophy that made British Columbia, in the 1960's, probably the most rapidly expanding of all the provinces in the Dominion, with Vancouver as its most energetic metropolis.

It would appear that the Trudeau Administration is on its way out, that Canada, after the manner of the United States, may be moving toward a more conservative electorate, and that social services and other swollen government outlays may be reduced to a more appropriate percentage of annual government income. It is entirely proper that the Dominion authorities be concerned about excessive alien control of Canadian resources, but equally they should be mindful that their country, even today, is largely underdeveloped and that significant capital funds from outsiders will be needed for required growth. Also, it should be remembered that Americans, for most of this century, have been welcomed not only as investors but as the best customers for a diversity of Canada's major products: wood pulp, paper, petroleum, natural gas, uranium, alcoholic beverages, grains, meat, asbestos, copper, lead, zinc, gold and silver. It's not a very bright long-range policy to be studiously unfriendly to your closest neighbor, your best customer, your military ally, and your most dependable banker!

Assuming, then, that the Canadian business and investment attitude toward Americans with surplus funds may improve in 1977, what are some of the specific securities

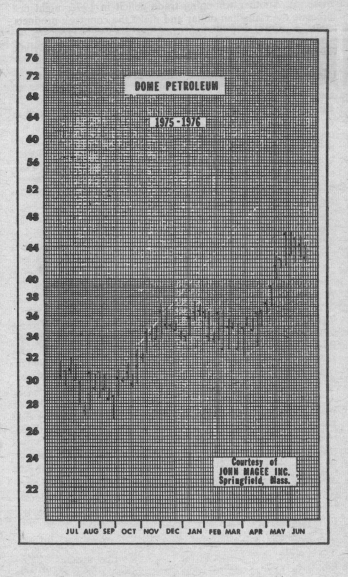

DOME PETROLEUM

1975-1976

Courtesy of
JOHN MAGEE INC.
Springfield, Mass.

that should be on a shopping list for those in quest of speculative gain?

A lead-off candidate would probably be Dome Petroleum. It is a fast growing company whose shares, up to this time, have not adequately reflected in market price either its profits or its potentials. Dome has been steadily expanding and developing petroleum properties and is an important producer of oil and natural gas in West Canada. About 17 percent of 1975 revenues were derived from oil and gas sales, 6 percent from pipeline income, and 75 percent from propane, ethane, and related hydrocarbon production.

Important in any consideration of Dome are its extensive working interests: 42,311,000 gross acres (21.2 million net) of gas and oil rights, plus 34,363,000 gross royalty acres. Approximately 65 percent of these interests lie on the Canadian East Coast and in the Arctic Islands. Recoverable reserves have been estimated at approximately 110 million (gross) barrels of oil and natural gas liquids, and over 1.8 billion MCF of natural gas.

The most significant current project of Dome is its exploration of some 2.3 million offshore acres, in conjunction with 3.5 million acres held by Hunt Oil Company, in the Beaufort Sea. This involves a startup investment of $120 million. (These funds have already been arranged via a 10-year loan with a group of Canadian banks.)

Dome is also a 50 percent owner of a fully integrated NGL pipeline system, complete with extraction plants, transmission lines and storage tanks. Dome is a large exporter of ethane and propane to the United States and has under way a project with Dow Chemical to build a twin pipeline to transport these products, in Canada, to the United States border.

Growth at Dome has been impressive, with sales rising from $41.5 million in 1971 to $235 million in 1975. In the same period, earnings per-share expanded from $1 to $3.65.

Capitalization is $239.7 million in long-term debt and 11,250,918 shares of common, 26.4 percent owned by Dome Mines, Ltd. Through a recent interchange of shares, Dome Petroleum now owns 9.3 percent of Dome Mine shares and thus has a stake in the production of gold and other minerals.

Dome Petroleum common, trading on NYSE under symbol DMP, may prove attractive at a price around 38 because of (1) its control of large exploration acreage; (2) its growth rate in both sales and profits; (3) the possibility of dividends. (So far no cash dividends have been paid, although there was a 3 for 1 stock split in 1971.)

If Dome strikes fortunately in the Beaufort Sea, its common shares might advance quite spectacularly.

Our view is that petroleum exploration must be expanded in Canada and funds made available for that purpose because: (1) Canada needs more oil to become self-sufficient; (2) United States demands for Canadian oil, gas, ethane, and propane are urgent; (3) higher prices are in the offing for all these products.

While Dome appears the lead stock, Scurry Rainbow might move well from a current quotation of 16. Others in the Canadian oil picture include Ashland Oil, Canadian Superior, Home Oil, Imperial Oil (Exxon affiliate), Texaco Canada, Ltd., Shell Canada, and Ranger Oil, a speculation with quite a stake in the North Sea. Ranger is perhaps the most potentially explosive stock in the list.

The long-range opportunities for gainful investment in Canada indeed appear attractive, and would be measurably improved by the arrival on the scene of a new and more conservative Prime Minister. Meanwhile, a rising world demand for oil and gas exists, as well as for major metals (in which Canada excels), with price trends in these commodities headed visibly upward.

Placer Development (23 on AMEX) is a splendid cash-rich company. Placer is the second largest molybdenum producer in North America. This stock may not double but it should perform quite well in 1977.

In minerals and mineral shares, desirable investment situations surely exist, limited somewhat by the rising costs of mine labor and equipment. We have earlier referred to certain interesting copper shares—Falconbridge, Gibraltar, and Texasgulf, which has a fabulous Canadian copper mine. More recently, another American company, Moore & McCormack Resources, has staked out a large copper property in Quebec.

Lead is another ascending metal. Lacana Mining has interesting Canadian lead and copper deposits, as well as Mexican silver. Cominco, Inc., the mineral affiliate of Canadian Pacific, is a very large lead producer and has a splendid across-the-board call on precious and nonferrous metals; it is always on the prowl for new ore bodies.

In nickel, International Nickel and Falconbridge Nickel

are the premier entries, both well managed and loaded with ore. Alcan is the dominant aluminum maker. A company called Continental Copper, selling around 60¢ as this was written, has been much talked about—not for its copper, however, so much as for its phosphate deposits in Ontario.

In gold and silver, we've mentioned in an earlier chapter such issues as Agnico-Eagle, Dome and Campbell, and Red Lake. Others might include Camflo and Kerr-Addison and Belmoral Mines, recently financed by some $4 million in French capital. (The French will never give up on gold!) We are less impressed with Canadian steel and iron ore companies. In asbestos, the big one is Asbestos, Ltd., listed on the Montreal Stock Exchange.

A special aura of mining romance—set off by the uranium boom that began in 1953—has attached to Canadian uranium mining, and many swift fortunes were made in this mineral in 1956–58. Canada is the leading foreign nation in uranium production, with some 760,000 tons that could be delivered at current prices of $40 a ton.

The Canadian uranium scene has been dominated by Denison Mines, Ltd. (Toronto Exchange) and Rio Algom Mines, Ltd. (ASE, 33). The Denison mill has a capacity of 7,000 tons a day and should handle approximately 1.4 million tons in 1976. Denison is a classy earner—$5.80 a share in 1975. While uranium is its specialty, Denison also has important holdings in oil and gas, West Canada coal acreage, and a building products subsidiary—Lake Ontario Cement Company. Although high priced, Denison shares are attractive because (1) they may be split; (2) 1976 profits should increase; and (3) the price for uranium has been in a long-term upswing, as nuclear power is becoming more and more the solution to our fuel problem.

Rio Algom plans a mill expansion to 7,000 tons a day (same as Denison). Its earnings from uranium are supplemented by a 66 percent ownership of Lornex Mining Corporation, Ltd., operating a British Columbia copper molybdenum open pit mine with fabulous reserves, enough to feed the 45,000 ton a day mill for a quarter century. Another kicker in Algom is its 10 per cent interest in the Rossing Mine in South Africa, probably the largest uranium mine in the world. Mention was made earlier of Inexco, Inc., whose Canadian subsidiary has a one-third slice of a new uranium ore body discovered not in the traditional areas at Elliot

Lake or Blind River but at Key Lake in northern Saskatchewan.

United Keno has been a much talked about silver company, but it has the disadvantage of a running-out ore body and property location far to the North where labor and other operating costs are higher and transportation charges to and from the outskirts of civilization are a factor.

Another, but smaller, silver mine is Dankoe in British Columbia. (Currently $2.45 on the Vancouver Exchange.)

While Canada still appears as the most desirable foreign haven for American investment capital, for bold risk-takers mindful of political uncertainties, other nations also afford interesting opportunities: Rosario Resources, for example, has rich mines of silver and gold in the Dominican Republic. A little company called Norsul (OTC $1.00) has a lively cut at Ecuadorian oil, sharing in a venture managed jointly by Texaco/Gulf. Nord Resources (OTC 7¾) has mineral operations in Africa, Brazil, Canada, and the United States. Rutile—a mineral consisting of titanium dioxide and iron—is its major product at this time. But of course, in spite of the occasional killing that can be made abroad, the best and safest investments for Americans will for the most part be in American industries.

Chapter XIII

The Roundup

This book, in common with most that relate to stock market decisions, has an unavoidable battle with time. Certain figures, particularly price quotations, are inevitably out of date by the time the book goes to press. For example, a stock selling at 20 when the text was prepared, with a fair prospect of doubling in value, may be selling at 26 when the book reaches you. What, then, should be your attitude? You have three rather obvious options: (1) you can buy at the higher price, on the assumption that the issue will advance further toward, and possibly reach, the original goal; (2) you can put in an open order at a lower price (possibly around 20), hoping to buy if the market recedes; or (3) you can skip that issue and look for another stock on our list of hopefuls that may still be available near its original quotation. If a stock suggested has meanwhile gone down in price, your decision is less difficult to make.

TWO SCHOOLS OF INVESTMENT ANALYSIS

There are two main schools of investment analysis in the market community today: those who use a fundamental approach to security selection, purchase, or sale; and those who favor the "technical" approach. The distinction between these two methods of decision-making are derived from divergent opinions as to the nature of the market itself. The fundamentalists' view is that market action is primarily a logical phenomenon—that individual stocks vary in price because of changes in basic conditions within each company. The fundamentalist, in determining the merit or attractiveness of a corporate stock, examines, analyzes, and constantly reviews: gross revenues, net earnings, profit margins, earnings on stockholders' equity, capital structure (particularly ratio of debt to equity and of current assets to current liabilities), cash flow, inventory position, tax status, dividend record, the trend of earnings and growth rates, plant facilities, and management capability.

This statistical analysis of securities presumes that, if the sales, profits, margins, dividends, and net worth of a company are steadily improving, the market may logically be expected to reflect this improvement in higher price quotations. The theory might be summarized in the phrase, "Stock prices are the slaves of earning power."

Our own view is that the stock market is a mixed phenomenon motivated about 60 percent of the time logically and 40 percent of the time psychologically. At the height, or near the crest of a bull market, or at depression levels, emotions take over and exert a powerful influence over investment decision, market activity, and direction. Quotations will then reflect sensitively either hope and confidence, or fear and panic. Such emotional reactions at these high or low extremes pervade the entire market—the good stocks go up or down with the bad, following the mood of the herd, and the underlying or comparative values of securities are to a great extent lost sight of in the stampede.

It is in these periods of high confidence or deep gloom, and particularly when market sentiment is reversing, that the "technical" approach to buying and selling would seem especially useful. The technicians believe that the action of the stock market itself is a quite reliable barometer or indicator of future prices, and that the whole market, as well as the prices for individual stocks, move in trends. The technical analyst scrutinizes actual trading in graphic form, through charts that depict the record of trading, price changes and volume of transactions in individual stocks, or in groups of stocks, such as the Dow-Jones 30 Industrials, or Standard & Poor's 500 stocks. The pattern of this market history as revealed by the charts is believed to foretell the probable price trend in the future.

The technical analyst may use several kinds of charts, some quite sophisticated. The most common variety is the daily chart of individual stocks that keeps a running account of the daily high and low (called "the range"), the daily volume, and the closing price. On these charts a vertical line connects the high and low, and a small horizontal bar indicates the closing price. Volume is shown by a vertical line drawn in the bottom section of the chart. The upper (price) line and the volume line give the history and tell the market story of each stock. In due course the price line may change direction. This is called a "reversal" and is highly significant.

What happens next is most revealing to the chartist. He has a series of formulations that give him messages about the immediate future behavior of the issue under study. There are such occult patterns as "head and shoulder" tops (or bottoms), triangles, rectangles, diamonds and a selling climax. All of this, and a great deal more, is splendidly presented in a book called *Technical Analysis of Stock Trends* by Robert D. Edwards and John Magee. (Mr. Magee, a dean among technicians and Susan MacFarlane are responsible for all of the charts in this book. If technical analysis interests you, the Edwards/McGee book is recommended reading.)

Our opinion of the relative merits of these two schools is mixed. Some truly remarkable projections of stock trends have been made by several brilliant chartists. The fundamental financial data on each corporation, on the record, has consistently revealed the intrinsic merits of common stocks and has led to rewarding purchases, as well as to timely sales, depending on the statistical evidence of a sustained rise or fall in net profits.

We have also seen some excellent selections by investment advisory services, institutions, and stock exchange houses that have reached their conclusions by combining or blending both approaches. The winnowing of securities in this book relies mainly on statistical (fundamental) data, but a reference, to or cross-check with, the chart on any particular stock is desirable for guidance in the timing of purchase or sale. If, for example, the earnings and financial position of a stock, say Control Data, are improving and the chart on the issue points to an indicated price uptrend and evidence of "accumulation," then your decision to buy would be doubly fortified.

The fundamentalists provide a logical reason to take action, while technical charts serve to clue you in on the "mood" of the market. Technical charts are no doubt less effective in the case of modest OTC stocks which trade only a few hundred shares a day than in evaluating shares of a great corporation trading in thousands of shares daily. The existence of an army of stockholders insures a good volume of activity, making possible a more accurate definition of a price trend.

Another and perhaps whimsical cross-check on the market

is the Odd-Lot theory, which is supposed to reveal price trends because the small odd-lot buyer historically has always been wrong. If he sells, the market is likely to advance! If he buys, it's headed down.

Many investors refer to the Barron's Confidence Index, which contrasts the yield of high-grade bonds with that of low-grade bonds. When "the interest spread" between these fixed income securities widens, it is bearish; when it narrows, it is bullish, because investors display more confidence. When people pay higher prices for low-grade bonds, it means they are more confident that interest on them will continue to be paid.

DIVERSIFICATION

A great deal has been written about the need for diversification—not putting all your eggs in one basket. If your goal is maximized diversification, then buy a mutual fund! One with $500 million invested may own 250 or 300 different issues of stocks.

Our thinking is that diversification has been overdone and often becomes little more than "scatterfication!" If you have screened and analyzed individual securities properly, you should be assembling a superior group and have less need to diversify than if you had bought at random. In a portfolio up to $100,000, you need no more than eight good issues; and no more than twenty or twenty-five for a $500,000 portfolio. The more you diversify, the less confidence you must have in the securities you've selected. Limit your holdings to a group small enough to follow closely, and weed out and replace the ones that don't live up to their billings after a suitable time interval. The purpose of diversification is: (1) to spread capital over a series of promising situations, and (2) not to have one issue, however promising, turn sour and represent such a high percentage of invested funds as to be disastrous. Even elegant company stocks can dive: Penn Central which paid dividends for 120 years dived in a decade from 86½ to 1; Avon Products went from 140 to 8½; G. D. Searle from 40¼ to 11⅜; and Simplicity Pattern Company from 58⅞ to 6½.

When to Sell

Something should surely be said about when to sell stock. Since the issues reviewed in the preceding pages are all presumed to be bought for capital gain, plans should be made well in advance for sale—in part or in entirety—at an appropriate time. There are, of course, no absolutes about sales timing, but here are a few guidelines:

1. Whenever a stock sells at a P/E ratio above 40, it is suspect and should in most cases be sold, particularly if it has climbed from much lower multiples within a short time.

2. When a growth type stock reports flat earnings, or a downtrend in three consecutive quarters, it has probably lost its growth characteristics, may be heading downward, and should be sold. The market respects only growth stocks that keep growing.

3. Often a stock is "a sale" right after announcement of a split. It may languish in price for several months.

4. "Sell when the clamor of the bulls is loudest." It is notorious that a horde of speculators, motivated by mass psychology, climb aboard markets near their tops. When everybody believes the market is going up, it's time to sell!

5. Sell when an important adverse change has taken place in a company. Several drug shares acted badly after their products were cited for harmful side effects. Carter Wallace slumped when its patent for Milltown expired; AMF and Brunswick descended after the bowling craze had peaked; motor home shares declined when the gas shortage hit, utility stocks faded when interest rates soared.

6. When a given stock has reached the price objective you had set, sell; but do not use an historic high as a target point. It may never reach that point again.

7. Don't sell, however, on dramatic incidents (except declaration of war). The market dips when the President of the United States dies, when a disturbing and warlike event occurs, and when disasters—floods, droughts, earthquakes—occur. But most of these will cause only a short run flutter, and the market will again resume its course after 60 or 90 days.

8. Never buy or sell on tips. Have an excellent reason for every market decision you make.

9. Sell if you need the money; but always sell the

poorest stocks first. (Most people sell the issue in which they have the most profit.)

10. Sell (or buy) at the market, except in OTC transactions where the market is thin and a specified price is necessary.

11. Don't sell in panic.

About buying:

1. Again, buy at the market, and don't miss the ownership of a stock by picayune "fractionitis"—trying to buy an eighth cheaper.

2. Don't buy on tips.

3. Don't follow a stock down. If you buy an issue and it sells off, either (a) conclude you've made a mistake and get rid of it, or (b) decide the decline is unwarranted and hold. Don't buy more just because it's cheaper, don't buy merely because the issue is near an all time low. It may belong there!

4. In general, set a buying unit that creates proper diversification. If your portfolio is $20,000, don't buy $8,000 of one issue. Limit it to $3,000 tops.

5. Avoid troubled companies.

6. Stress companies in strong financial position.

7. Don't hurry to buy after a management change.

And now, since this is a roundup chapter, we'd like to take up a few subjects that didn't fit into previous chapters but which are worth discussing before you brace yourself and take the plunge into the section of potential doublers.

CONVERTIBLES

In this book we have not covered convertibles because: (1) they have been well presented in many other publications on investment; (2) they merely reflect the prices of the related common stock (so why not buy the stocks directly?); (3) they confuse decision making when they sell at high premiums; (4) people can get careless and hold convertibles until the privilege has expired.

The presumed virtues of "converts" are that: (1) they go up parallel to the common stock but are more protective on the down side; (2) they are better collateral; (3) they may pay a higher return than the stock; (4) brokerage costs are less.

Accepting these virtues, our view is that if you are considering a common stock in a company that has a "convert," then look at and analyze the "convert" and possibly buy it if: (1) it does not sell at too high a premium (over 15 percent) over conversion value; (2) yields more than the common stock; (3) has an active market; (4) does not *sell* at a high premium over par value (such as 150). After you buy, sell the convert if you've made a good profit, and look for another lower-priced issue. Don't convert into the stock. Buy convertible bonds rather than convertible preferred stocks. The best time to buy converts is before the privilege has become valuable. This way you get the relative safety of the bond, a good interest return and are given a speculative "kicker" for practically nothing.

VISION

The Book of Proverbs has a wonderful quotation: "Where there is no vision, the people perish." Keep your eyes open if you want to make a killing in the market! Look for some new situation or development that may prove profitable: coal stocks in a time of oil shortage; new drugs or medical instruments (such as pacemakers); new food trends (pizza parlors, convenience foods); new apparel trends and the companies identified with them (Levi Strauss for denim wear); communication advances (Comsat, stereos, and now, Citizen Band transceivers); innovations such as ball point pens, crock pot cookery (which boosted Rival Manufacturing Company); leisure pastimes (look at the growth of Franklin Mint with its coins and medallions).

New ideas, products, and services require judgment, however, because some novelties die in a hurry: hula hoops, miniature golf. Old products can phase out too: men's garters, felt hats, derbies, women's corsets, high shoes. Some products come back with a bang, like denim. For decades, this fabric was limited to work clothes for mill hands, mechanics and plow boys. Who would ever have thought of going to a party in a denim dinner jacket!

Nothing in investment beats early perception of a major industrial trend or breakthrough—early purchase of Xerox, Polaroid, IBM, Kentucky Fried Chicken, Tropicana, McDonald's, Disney, 3M. We've listed a number of innovative companies in this book, and we believe we've gone further than any other stock market author in attempting to target for you the future Xeroxes and Polaroids. The rest is up to you.

We'd like to end on another investment note. Many of the stocks cited here, if they perform as advertised, will advance nicely and eventually you'll sell them. What will you do with the money? Here's a final list of stocks in which to salt away your profits on a fairly permanent basis. Good comfortable long-term holdings that won't require too much surveillance but that should continue to enhance in value. We don't expect them to double in a year, but we do expect them to perform in a superior manner for many, many years to come.

A Selection of Serene Stocks
Amax Corporation
Standard Oil of California
St. Joe Minerals
Texas Utilities
Coca-Cola
American Home Products
S.S. Kresge
Columbia Broadcasting
Connecticut General Life
American Tel and Tel
Nortrust
Southern Railway
Squibb
Toledo Edison

These are all beautifully managed companies, money-makers for years, and dependable dividend-payers. They have good growth factors, and are all among the best in their fields.

And so, the ball is now in your court. If you are not an expert in the stock market, at least you have, in reading this book, taken advantage of the expertise of someone who, if we may boast a bit, has an excellent track record.

Review the salient general points. Then concentrate on the individual stocks discussed in the book. Perhaps a bit of psychology will come into play. An eminent psychologist insists that, when one is scanning a menu, he should order the first dish that leaps out at him—because that is the one his stomach wants him to eat.

The chances are that, as you review these stocks, several will "leap out at you." Back up your reaction with a more detailed study of those particular stocks. Then if your investigation confirms your hunch, these could well be the very selections that bring you the happiness of a stock that doubles in a year! Good luck.

Glossary

ACCRUED INTEREST: The interest on a bond, note or debenture which has been earned since the last interest payment thereon.

AMERICAN STOCK EXCHANGE: Sometimes called "the Curb," the second major securities exchange in New York.

AMEX: Abbreviation for above.

AMORTIZATION: The "writing off" of an asset over a period of time, usually at a certain annual percentage.

ANALYST: A professional evaluator of securities and economic trends.

ANNUAL REPORT: The official statement of assets, liabilities, earnings and net worth and progress (if any), of a corporation, covering a fiscal or calendar year.

ARBITRAGE: Taking advantage of existing price differentials by simultaneous buying and selling (usually in different markets) of identical or intrinsically equivalent assets (currencies, commodities or securities).

ASSETS: Anything a corporation owns or is owed.

AVERAGES: The various barometers of stock price trends. Best known are the Dow Jones Industrial Average, made up of thirty major stocks; N.Y. Times Average of fifty stocks; Standards and Poor's Average of four hundred twenty-five Industrial Stocks; NYSE Common Stock Index, a composite of all "listed" common stocks.

BANKRUPTCY: Where a corporation's liabilities exceed its assets and it is unable to meet its current obligations. There are two kinds: Chapter XI, Voluntary—where an accommodation with creditors may be worked out, and Chapter X, Involuntary—where assets under court order are placed in the hands of a referee for disposition to satisfy creditors (usually but not always).

BALANCE SHEET: A financial statement revealing the assets, liabilities, capital and net worth of a company on a specific date.

BEAR: A person who thinks stocks are going down; and may sell stock "short" to back up his opinion.

BEAR MARKET: A declining one.

BID AND ASKED: A quotation of the best price which will be paid, and the lowest priced offering of a security at a given moment.

BIG BOARD: The New York Stock Exchange.

BLUE CHIP: The common stock of a major company, with a long record of earnings and dividends.

BLUE SKY LAWS: Laws in many states protecting investors against being sold a slice of "the blue sky," i.e., a fraudulent, mythical or misrepresented security.

BOARD ROOM: Sitting room for stock traders in a broker's office.

BOILER ROOM: A place where second-rate or worthless securities are sold to the gullible—usually over the phone.

BOND: The long-term obligation of a corporation to repay a given sum (usually in $1,000 denominations) on a given date, with a specified rate of interest to be paid at regular intervals until then. Bonds can be debentures (unsecured), or protected by collateral, lien, or mortgage on corporate property.

BOND PRICES: Quotations, given as percentages of par value.

BOOK VALUE: All the assets of a company, less all liabilities and the par value of preferred stocks (if any) divided by the number of common shares outstanding.

BROKER: A financial agent associated with a member of a stock exchange or a broker/dealer firm, who executes orders in securities or commodities on a commission basis.

BULL: A person believing that the market will rise, and aiming to profit if it does.

CALLABLE: A bond or preferred stock that may be redeemed and retired under certain conditions, and at a specified price.

CALL OPTION: A contract to buy 100 shares of a stock at a specified price, for a limited period of time.

CAPITAL ASSETS: The fixed assets of a company, a factory, office building, plant, warehouse, trucks, etc.

CAPITAL GAIN OR LOSS: Profit or loss realized when a security (or other asset) is sold.

CAPITAL STOCK: The shares which represent the ownership of, or equity in, a company.

CAPITALIZATION: The entire amount of all securities (debt and equity) issued by a corporation.

CASH FLOW: The net income of a company (for a given period) to which are added depletion, depreciation, amortization charges; and non-recurring charges to reserves; frequently stated "per share."

CATS AND DOGS: Low priced stocks of dubious worth.

CBOE: Chicago Board Option Exchange.

CHARTS: Statistical data about prices, volume and trends in different stocks, portrayed graphically, hopefully to indicate the future direction of prices.

COLLATERAL: Property, most frequently securities, pledged to secure interest and repayment of a loan.

COMMISSION: The fee charged by a broker to execute an order to buy or sell.

COMMON STOCKS: The ownership or equity interest in a corporation, with a claim on assets or earnings, coming after preferred stocks, notes, bonds, or other indebtedness.

CONGLOMERATE: A company which has accumulated as subsidiaries a group of companies in many different and unrelated lines of business.

CONTROL: The group owning enough stock (customarily 51 percent or more), or influencing enough stockholders, to direct the affairs of a corporation.

CONVERTIBLE: A bond or preferred stock, which may, under certain conditions, be exchanged for common stock, usually in the same company.

CORPORATION: A legally organized intangible organization operating (usually) under a state charter with: (1) unlimited life, (2) limited liability, and (3) transferable certificates representing shares of ownership.

COUPON BOND: One which pays interest semi-annually, by means of detachable coupons which can be cashed when due.

CUMULATIVE PREFERRED: A stock which may pay at a later date any omitted regular dividends, and on which all past due dividends must be paid before the common stock can receive any distribution.

CUSTOMER'S MAN: A representative of a stock exchange firm.

CURRENT ASSETS: Assets in cash, receivables, short term securities, and items collectible and convertible into cash within a year.

CURRENT LIABILITIES: What a company owes that must be paid within a year.

CUT A MELON: To declare a substantial extra dividend, usually in stock.

CYCLICAL STOCKS: Those whose earnings tend to fluctuate with the business cycle.

DEBENTURE: A kind of bond, unsecured by lien or mortgage on any specific property.

DELISTED: When a security is removed from trading on a stock exchange, and reverts to the OTC market.

DEPLETION: A bookkeeping charge against earnings to mark the lower remaining value of a natural resource holding (coal, oil, minerals, timber) after some part of it has been removed, extracted or exhausted.

DEPRECIATION: A bookkeeping charge against earnings to write down the cost of an asset over its useful life.

DIRECTOR: A person elected by company shareholders to be a member of its Board of Directors, and a maker of corporate policies and decisions.

DIVERSIFICATION: The spreading of investments among many different securities and industries.

DIVIDEND: A payment authorized by a Board of Directors either in cash or in stock, pro rata among shareholders. Usually a distribution made from current or past profits.

DOLLAR COST AVERAGING: Applying a level sum of money each year, say, $1,000, to the purchase of as many shares of a stock as those dollars will buy at then prevailing prices.

DOW THEORY: An attempt to project market trends on the basis of the correlated past market action of 30 industrial and 20 transportation stocks.

ECONOMIST: A social scientist, often in error, but seldom in doubt.

EQUITY: The interest in a company represented by ownership of either (or both) its common or preferred stock.

EX DIVIDEND (X): Indicates that the stock, if bought, does not carry with it the dividend most recently declared.

EXTRA: Any declaration in stock or cash above regular or customary dividend distribution.

FEDERAL RESERVE BOARD: The quasi-government agency controlling the supply and price of money and regulating installment credit and margin loans.

FISCAL YEAR: The official accounting year of a corporation

(usually), when it does not coincide with the calendar year.

FIXED CHARGES: Fixed expenses of a corporation which must be paid whether earned or not—most commonly interest charges, or rentals.

FLOOR: The trading area on a stock exchange.

FUNDAMENTAL ANALYSIS: Evaluation of a stock on the basis of its earnings, assets, profit margins, dividends and investment stature.

FUNDED DEBT: Long term interest bearing obligations of a company, most commonly bonds and debentures.

GILT EDGED: A high grade bond, so called because it referred originally to issues payable (before 1933) in dollars convertible into gold.

GOING PUBLIC: The public offering of a company's securities for the first time.

GROWTH STOCK: A company whose sales, earnings, and net worth are expanding at an unusual rate.

GTC: An order good until cancelled (or executed).

INSIDER: A person or corporation owning 10 percent or more of the stock of a public company, who must report to S.E.C. each month any substantial changes in holdings.

INTEREST: The price paid for use or rental of money, expressed as a percentage per annum.

INVESTMENT BANKER: An individual or a firm buying securities for resale to others. Also called an underwriter.

INVESTMENT COUNSEL: An individual or firm paid a fee to advise and/or manage investment accounts.

INVESTMENT TRUST: A company which gathers funds from individuals, and which invests these funds in a portfolio of diversified securities, professionally managed. There are "open end" trusts (called mutual funds) whose outstanding shares vary in number from day to day.

LAMB: A gullible investor.

LEVERAGE: Using other people's money to generate earnings or gain for you, as when large amounts of senior securities exist in a corporate capitalization, ahead of its common stock. Leverage is also created by using borrowed money to buy stocks (or a house with a mortgage).

LIABILITIES: Any and all legal claims against a company.

LIEN: A mortgage or other legal claim against property to secure a debt.

LISTED STOCK: Shares trading on any stock exchange (most

commonly the New York, American, and regional stock exchanges).

LONG: Means that you own a specific security or securities; as opposed to a short position where you sell what you don't own.

MANAGEMENT: The officers of a company and the board of directors which elects them.

MANIPULATION: The illegal "rigging" of stock prices by artificial stimulation sometimes involving the spread of incorrect information.

MARGIN: The use of money borrowed from a broker in the purchase of securities.

MARGIN CALL: Broker's request for more money on margined securities in a declining market.

MARKET ORDER: An order to buy or sell at the best obtainable price then prevailing.

MERGER: When two or more companies are joined together.

MUTUAL FUND: See "Investment Trusts."

MUNICIPALS: A generic term for bonds issued by counties, cities, states, districts or public authorities, usually with the interest payments exempt from Federal taxation.

NEW YORK STOCK EXCHANGE: The world's leading auction market for securities.

NYSE: Abbreviation for above.

NEW ISSUE: The first public offering of a bond or stock.

ODD LOT: A small amount of stock, customarily less than 100 shares.

OVER-THE-COUNTER: The largest, and a nationwide, telephone and electronic market for those securities not regularly traded on any exchange.

OTC: Abbreviation for above.

PAPER PROFIT: Unrealized indicated gain on a security still held.

PAR VALUE: Face or nominal value of a security.

PENNY SHARES: Customarily those selling at $1.00 or less.

PERFORMANCE STOCK: One that gains spectacularly in price (or is expected to!).

PER SHARE NET: Total net earnings of a company after taxes, for a given period, divided by the number of common shares outstanding.

POINT: A point is $1.00 on stocks, or $10 on a bond.

PORTFOLIO: The total security holdings of an individual or institution.

PRIME RATE: The interest rate charged by banks to their best customers on unsecured loans.

PREFERRED STOCK: A stock having a claim on a company's earnings or assets, ahead of its common stock, and usually entitled to dividends at a fixed rate.

PREMIUM: The amount by which a bond or preferred stock sells above its face amount; or a new issue sells above its offering price.

PRINCIPAL: A person or firm who buys and sells for his own account.

PRICE/EARNINGS RATIO: The current price of a stock, divided by the per share net earnings of the issuing company, for the most recently reported 12 month period. (Also called "P/E Multiple.")

PROSPECTUS: A summary of all the pertinent history, facts and figures about a company and the people who run it, prior to a new securities offering. By law, a prospectus must be presented to a possible buyer in advance of any purchase.

PROXY: Designation, by a stockholder, of someone else to represent him at a stockholder's meeting.

PUTS AND CALLS: Options to buy (a call), or to sell (a put), a certain number of shares of a stock at fixed prices for limited periods of time.

QUOTATION: The bid and asked price of a security.

RED HERRING: An early prospectus draft, omitting the offering price of the issue.

REGISTERED REPRESENTATIVE: A person approved by the Stock Exchange to handle orders for the purchase or sale of securities for clients. Also called an Account Executive and, formerly, a Customer's Man or Customer's Broker.

REFINANCING: The issuance of new securities to refund outstanding ones or to retire or extend a debt.

REGISTRATION: The filing of information about a forthcoming security offering with the Securities and Exchange Commission (national regulatory body) preliminary to preparation and printing of a prospectus.

RIGHTS: The privilege, given to a shareholder, to buy additional stock in a company for a limited time and at a special price.

S.E.C.: The Securities and Exchange Commission, a Federal organization for the regulation of the securities industry.

SECONDARY DISTRIBUTION: Offering of securities, previously issued, in which the company receives no share of the proceeds.

SENIOR SECURITIES: Bonds, notes and preferred stocks ranking ahead of common stock.

SHORT SALE: Selling stock sold "short" (that is, not owned) with a view to buying it back later at a lower price; the stock is borrowed for delivery meanwhile (usually from a broker).

SINKING FUND: Money reserved by a corporation to buy in, and redeem, its own senior securities.

STOP ORDER: An instruction to sell when and if a security reaches a certain price.

SPECIALIST: A floor member of an exchange designated to maintain an orderly market in specified securities and to act as a broker's broker.

SPECULATION: The employment of funds and assumption of risks primarily to create capital gains.

SPIN-OFFS: The delivery by a parent company to its stockholders of shares in another corporation.

SPLIT: Increasing the outstanding number of shares in a company by division of the existing ones.

STOCK DIVIDEND: A dividend paid not in cash but in securities.

STREET NAME: Stock held in the name of a broker or nominee instead of the legal owner.

SWEETENER: A convertible privilege or a warrant attached to a senior security to make the issue more attractive and to thus reduce its interest or dividend rate.

SYNDICATE: A group of security firms cooperating with the underwriting firm in the distribution of a security issue.

TAX EXEMPT BOND: One with its interest payments exempt from Federal income taxation.

TECHNICAL ANALYSIS: Evaluation of stocks on the basis of their recent market performance, volume and price trends.

THIN MARKET: One in which there are few bids and offerings and (often) wide "spreads" between them.

TICKER: The electric device which immediately reports and transmits on tape prices and volumes of security transactions.

TIPS: Confidential urgings to buy certain securities, supposed to be based on information "from the horse's mouth."

TRADING POST: U-shaped booths on the floor of the NYSE, each one assigned to trade about 75 different stocks.

TRADING SYMBOLS: The abbreviations containing no more than three letters for listed stocks; sometimes four for OTC issues.

TRANSFER: The official recording of change in ownership of a security, performed by a transfer agent.

TREASURY STOCK: Stock formerly outstanding but repurchased by the company.

UNLISTED: (See Over-the-Counter) Name given to those securities not listed on any exchange but traded over-the-counter.

UTILITIES: A broad classification of corporate monopolies, including gas, electric, telephone and water companies.

WARRANT: A certificate authorizing its owner to buy a share, shares (or fractions) of common stock of a company at a specific price and during a specified time period.

WHEN ISSUED: A security trading regularly but not available for actual delivery until some future date.

WIRE HOUSE: A NYSE member firm connected with its branch offices or correspondents by direct telephone or teletype circuits.

YIELD: The return on investment in a given security at its current price, expressed as a percentage. To determine the yield on a stock, divide the present indicated annual dividend by the market price of a single share.

Common Wall Street Abbreviations

These are the abbreviations most frequently used in stock and bond tables in the *Wall Street Journal* and daily newspaper financial sections.

a	Figure includes regular quarterly dividend plus one or more extra dividends
b	Annual rate plus stock dividend
c	Liquidating dividend
dd	Called
e	Paid last year
f	Payable in stock, with cash value of the distribution estimated
g	Declared or paid so far this year
h	Declared or payable after stock has split; or a capital distribution
N	New issue
P	Received or paid in a given year, plus stock dividend
c/d	Called
X	Ex-dividend
EX	Ex-distribution
XW	With warrants removed
WI	When issued
WW	With warrants
Nd	Next day delivery
vj	In bankruptcy, receivership or reorganization
F	Dealt in flat; i.e., without interest accrued
cts.	Certificates
St	Stamped
Fn	Foreign

Index

Boldface entries refer to stock analysis charts.

SIGNET and MENTOR Books of Interest

Other MENTOR Books You'll Want to Read

Books of Interest from MENTOR Executive Library

☐ **MODERN MANAGEMENT & MACHIAVELLI by Richard H. Buskirk.** An executive's guide to the psychology and politics of power, based on Machiavelli's classics **The Prince** and **The Discourses.** Machiavelli's practical advice on how to achieve success in a competitive world is applied directly to the day-to-day problems and challenges of modern management.
(#MJ1442—$1.95)

☐ **MANAGERS FOR TOMORROW by the staff of Rohrer, Hibler, and Replogle, edited by Charles D. Flory.** A team of highly qualified industrial psychologists and management consultants examine the characteristics of the successful executive in industry's increasingly complex managerial positions. Foreword by Clarence B. Randall, former president of Inland Steel.
(#MJ1592—$1.95)

☐ **HOW TO START AND MANAGE YOUR OWN BUSINESS by Gardiner G. Greene.** If you run a small business, you need all the help you can get—and this is the book that gives it all to you, with information on financial strategies, selecting professional services, developing and marketing your product, the psychology of negotiating, contracting with the government, and everything else you need to know to be your own boss, create your own company, and make a good profit!
(#MJ1409—$1.95)

☐ **CORPORATE ETIQUETTE by Milla Alihan.** Why do some executives quickly rise on the corporate ladder, while others, seemingly just as qualified, remain bogged down on the lower echelons? An eminent business consultant clearly spotlights all the trouble areas where minor gifts can turn into major roadblocks to advancement in this essential guide to getting ahead in the fast-changing business world of today.
(#MJ1304—$1.95)

THE NEW AMERICAN LIBRARY, INC.,
P.O. Box 999, Bergenfield, New Jersey 07621

Please send me the MENTOR BOOKS I have checked above. I am enclosing
$_____(check or money order—no currency or C.O.D.'s). Please
include the list price plus 35¢ a copy to cover handling and mailing costs.
(Prices and numbers are subject to change without notice.)

Name_____

Address_____

City_____ State_____ Zip Code_____
Allow at least 4 weeks for delivery

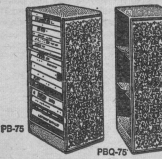

HANDY FILES AND CASES FOR STORING MAGAZINES, CASSETTES, & 8-TRACK CARTRIDGES

CASSETTE STORAGE CASES

Decorative cases, custom-made of heavy bookbinder's board, bound in Kid-Grain Leatherette, a gold-embossed design. Individual storage slots slightly tilted back to prevent handling spillage. Choice of: Black, brown, green.

#JC-30—30 unit size (13½x5½x6½") $11.95 ea.
3 for $33.00
#JC-60—60 unit size (13½x5½x12⅝") $16.95 ea.
3 for $48.00

MAGAZINE VOLUME FILES

Keep your favorite magazines in mint condition. Heavy bookbinder's board is covered with scuff-resistant Kivar. Specify the title of the magazine and we'll send the right size case. If the title is well-known it will appear on the spine in gold letters. For society journals, a brass-rimmed window is attached and gold foil included—you type the title.

#J-MV—Magazine Volume Files
$4.95 ea.
3 for $14.00
6 for $24.00

8-TRACK CARTRIDGE STORAGE CASE

This attractive unit measures 13¾ inches high, 6½ inches deep, 4½ inches wide, has individual storage slots for 12 cartridges and is of the same sturdy construction and decorative appearance as the Cassette Case.

#J-8T12—4½" wide (holds 12 cartridges)
$8.50 ea.
3 for $23.50
#J-8T24—8½" wide (holds 24 cartridges)
$10.95 ea.
3 for $28.00
#J-8T36—12¾" wide (holds 36 cartridges)
$14.25 ea.
3 for $37.00

Please send:

ITEM NO	COLOR (IF CHOICE)	DESCRIPTION	QUANTITY	UNIT PRICE	TOTAL COST

Postage and handling charges (up to $10 add $1.50) ($10.01 to $20 add $2.50) ($20.01 to $40 add $3.50)
(over $40 postage FREE)
I enclose ☐ check ☐ money order in amount of $ _____ Total _____

The New American Library, Inc.
P.O. Box 999
Bergenfield, New Jersey 07621

Name _____
Address _____
City _____ State _____ Zip _____

Offer valid only in the United States of America.   (Allow 5 weeks for delivery.)